The Chair Man

Life and times of John Lee, a Romany gypsy

As told to Angela Wigglesworth

New Generation Publishing

Books by the same author

Falkland People
People of Scilly
People of Wight
Lewes, a Photographic History of your Town

Preface

I first met John Lee in 2014. He was caning a chair for a friend of mine, and told her about his Romany gypsy childhood and the many challenging situations life had thrown at him. She thought it was such an unusual story it should be published, and mentioned it to me.

John came to my house and I learnt more about him. He was not a celebrity, a famous literary or political person, but he has had an extraordinary life that I, too, felt was well worth telling.

This is his story in his own words.

Angela Wigglesworth

To

ROSALIND

Tiffoy

John O'Lee

ii

Acknowledgements

My grateful thanks to David Arscott, Doug Morrison, Leo Nasskau and John Webber for their helpful proof reading, Kate Pool of the Society of Authors for her advice on contracts, Tony Tree for the generous use of his photographs, Chris Wigglesworth for his constructive advice and IT expertise, and Ann Cullen for encouraging me to write the book.

Dedicated to my grandparents who brought me up

CONTENTS

Chapter 1

Breaking the Romany bloodline. My grandparents.
My Romany childhood.

The event that had the most effect on my life happened the moment I was conceived. My family were Romany gypsies but my father was not. He was a French travelling salesman and I don't know how he and my mother met, but when she told her mother she was pregnant, that was taboo. 'You know what you've done to your baby,' her mother told her. 'You've cut his bloodline in half and he is going to have a terrible life. He won't be able to marry into a gypsy family or live on a Romany site.'

I was born in Suffolk on May 8th, 1930 and my father had already left. I never met him and he was never spoken about. When I was ten weeks old, my mother came in from working in the fields and my grandmother told her to leave her baby, pack her things and go. Which she did. They never spoke about her. Apparently she always knew this was coming because of what she'd done to me, but didn't know when. My grandparents brought me up.

They were proper Romany gypsies. My grandfather was Hungarian, a bare-fist knuckle fighter and a horse doctor, not an official one, but he knew all about horses and was an expert with a big long bull whip. If you had enough courage to stand with a cigar in your mouth, he could whip it out from twenty yards away. He could pick up a young horse from underneath, get the balance, then just lift it off the floor. He was a powerful man, not tall, about 5'6" but had a 54" chest, dark hair and eyes. And muscular, there was no fat on him, his big, strong legs were a bit like a body builder's. His wrist was like two of mine put together and his fingers were enormous. He always wore a suit with a stiff fly-away collar, braces and a belt and had a gold watch on a chain. His corduroy trousers had leather straps on them, the kind farmers used to wear when cutting hay so rats or mice wouldn't run up their legs.

I don't know too much about his younger days because he wouldn't talk about them, but I know the gentry used to go and watch his bare-fist knuckle fighting and there was a lot of money involved. One time he had a fight and the man died. It was all covered up but he had to leave Hungary. He never spoke about it and you couldn't question him. He would say that was then and this is now. Finished.

When he first arrived in Italy from Hungary, he had stowed away on a boat and stayed six months, going round different sites and sleeping rough. It was where he met my grandma. He had a couple of fights in Italy but I think the memories of killing the fella stopped him doing it and made him decide to come and live in England where my grandma had family. I think they felt there wasn't much in Italy for them. I also think that, when they decided that they were going to bring me up, I wasn't to know too much about his life.

Before they left Italy, my grandfather asked my grandma to marry him. She said 'yes' straight away. He was a quiet man, didn't have a lot to say to people, really preferred to be on his own. But he taught me about life and what it was going to be like for me, not able to live the gypsy way when they died, but to always remember that I was born a gypsy, to think like one and to live by my traditions and customs from down the generations. Which I have done and still do. He knew all about the way the *gorgers* (non-gypsies) lived because he mixed so much with them, buying and selling horses.

I always felt he was a bit hard on me. When we sat down at the table, if I had my elbow on it, he'd go, wallop, and push it off. 'Food to mouth, not mouth to food' he'd say. I always had to wear a napkin and I've still got the silver ring with my initials on it. Some times he'd flick me with his bull whip, I still have a scar from one occasion. I

2

think I was a boisterous child and a bit of a handful. I didn't take any notice of anyone. He'd say, 'You don't do that', and flick the whip.

I didn't see too much of him as he was away a lot. In those days, many of the streets were cobblestone and if he wanted to buy a horse, my grandfather would walk it up and down, listen to it and if one of its feet went *clip clong* instead of *clip clop*, he knew there was something wrong. He'd go round and touch its fetlock and if the horse jumped, he knew, just by touching that nerve, it had rheumatism. When he'd got enough money, he bought about three acres of land in Mitcham and built stables and tack rooms where he could keep the horses.

My feelings for my grandfather changed as I got older because I came to know him in a man's way. He was very strict about behaviour towards other people, you had to show them respect, be truthful and sincere and, if someone was a good friend, loyalty.

My grandmother who was Italian, was a lovely lady, about 5'6", a bit tubby but with a beautiful face, brown eyes and jet black hair. She always wore a dress with a smock, petticoat and a pinny. The elderly ladies used to wear money bags and I remember one day I was looking at her and said, 'You're putting a bit of weight on, grandma', and she said she wasn't. I said, 'You are' and to satisfy my curiosity, she lifted her skirt and there was a great big money belt tied round her full of £5 notes. She had a terrific sense of humour, a gentle person, very loving, very caring and would help anybody. If there was a young couple and they wanted to go out, she'd look after the baby. The gypsy children loved her. They would come and sit around her and ask her to tell them a story, which she always did. And when she'd finished, she'd ask them to sing her a gypsy song, which they did. She was a very well-loved woman.

She knew how I was going to be treated when they weren't there any more and I would have to live as a *gorger*. It was why she registered me at birth so I'd be able

3

to get a driving licence and a passport and things like that. It took a lot of paper work and a lot of people came to see her. She had to prove this and prove that. The Gypsy Council helped her – they agreed this would the best thing for me.

She was a hard worker. She had a round in Chelsea cleaning brass door knockers and fenders and she'd go mad if someone tried to go on her patch. She did chair caning, people brought them to her, it was all word of mouth. There were a lot of caners about then. Sometimes she'd go up to Box Hill with the horse and cart and pick wild lavender, which she'd strip off into a blanket. In them days, material shops left unused bits outside for the dustmen and she'd go round and collect them and make lavender bags to sell to the gentry. As far as I know, my grandfather never gave her any money but he brought her jewellery every time he came home from selling horses, specially when he went to Ireland. She loved china, too, and she had a cabinet full of beautiful pieces.

She could read and write a little though she didn't teach me, but she did teach me how to cane chairs and make clothes pegs from willow trees. They had to be nine and a half inches long and were tied at the end to stop the willow splitting. The trees grew wild as well as cultivated and I'd find a nice branch and cut a piece off. My grandma sold them with the lavender bags. We used to make the pegs and lavender bags of an evening in the *vada* (the gypsy word for wagon).

I didn't have a childhood like most children. When I was young, I was invited to play with others on the site until word got round that I was not a proper gypsy and then they weren't allowed to mix with me. 'He's a Pikey boy' (the gypsy word for a non-gypsy), they used to say. I'd play on my own near my grandma when she was caning chairs and, well, when you're seven you're going to fidget a bit and wander off, aren't you? Then she'd give me a wallop and say, 'Come here, boy, stand and watch, I'm teaching you how to get a living.' I started on my first chair when I was about eight and was doing one on my own when I was eleven. One night, she sat me down and spoke to me about how hard my life was going to be and not what it was like now. But it just didn't sink in. I thought I'd always be able to live like this. I never worried about anything and still don't.

They didn't have a lot of money and only one *vada*. I used to sleep underneath it on some straw with a canvas 'curtain' on one side and two lurchers used for hunting on the other. If you went anywhere near me, those dogs would have eaten you! My grandfather wasn't dubious about anything, but he was a bit cautious about them. He'd go, 'Come on boys' and they knew his voice, and they'd growl. I used to get into bed and put my arms round them, just the two of them and me, it was very warm. The thing that used to excite me about those dogs was to see them running after a hare. The way they could spin round on a sixpence and go off again, it was unbelievable. You wouldn't think a great big dog like that could do what they did. They'd catch the hare all right.

The family *vada* was very cosy and warm inside. The woodstove fire was on the left, there was always plenty of wood. If you looked at the back, it had three steps up and the fireplace was on the left so that smoke coming out of the chimney didn't blow on to the traffic coming behind. The china cabinet was on the right – Romany gypsies love china – and there were fold-up chairs and a table and bunk beds at the back: V*adas* are quite big inside. It had a stable door and two sets of leaded windows on each side and light came from Calor gas. There was always a great big copper kettle hanging over the fire, always on the boil and there'd be a hot drink if you wanted one. Sometimes my grandma bought things from the shops, but not food. She would get vegetables from the farmers and meat was plentiful, wild duck, hedgehog, wood pigeon, pheasant, squirrel, rabbit, wild pig, and there was fish from the streams.

When Romanies stay in the same place for a while they

grow vegetables and keep two or three chickens. They make jam from fruits in the hedgerows, and tea from dandelions, elderberries and nettles. They cook on a spit, take a patch of grass, dig a hole and stay for a few days to give the horses a bit of a rest. When they move on they put the turf back and you'd never know they'd been. For water, they fill two great barrels on the side of the *vadas,* which are quite heavy, for the horses to pull.

My grandmother used to make her own bread and get her own wheat, which she'd bang down on the table to take all the bits out. It used to take her hours. I'd watch her and today I'm not a bad cook myself. As well as being terrific cooks, the women make their own soap out of the marrow of animal bones and you can sometimes see the grandmothers grinding them down. They grind chestnuts too, because of the oil in them. Only a little drop is needed to make a pudding with it.

When I was nine, my grandfather bought me my own little *vada,* which was nice. He had it painted in the gypsy colours, yellow, green, red and brown, and I loved living in it. He was a very early riser. He'd come round at four or five in the morning, winter or summer, and say, 'Come on, boy, get your pyjamas off'. And he'd pick me up and drop me into one of the big water barrels. The water was always very cold. Since then, I've never been able to have a hot bath and if you put your hand in my bath water, you'd say, 'Oh, that's cold'. I can't have a hot shave either, but I can sit in the sun as hot as you like and it doesn't make no difference.

Chapter 2

Going to work. My first and only day at school.
Romany life.

I was working on the streets at thirteen. I'd get up in the morning and my grandma cooked breakfast – porridge and tea and maybe a bit of toast. She always made me eat something before I went out and sometimes gave me a sandwich to take for lunch.

I couldn't go to nearby places to work because the other guys from the site would go there so I'd take a train to Richmond. I was 'on the knocker', knocking on doors and asking if there were any chairs to be mended or if they'd like to buy some of the clothes pegs we'd made.

I was quite happy doing this. I loved sitting on the street, meeting people and I'd do good business. I think people felt sorry for me. I preferred to work outside because others would see what I was doing and I'd get more orders. I remember once in Beckenham, I knocked on a door and got a chair to mend and when I was doing it, a woman came up and asked if I could do something for her, which was painting the outside of her bungalow. I used to do all sorts of things, gardening, laying crazy pavements, repairing doors. In them days you could buy lovely tools, saws and chisels and things like that and I could make a door when I was fifteen. I'd found an old Victorian one, taken it to pieces and seen how it was made. I did anything people wanted doing and never said I couldn't do something because if I didn't know how to, I knew someone who'd tell me. I never refused any work.

I'd work all day until I'd made enough money or finished a chair. I tried to do a couple a day and that would make three shillings. Then I went home. I gave the money to my grandma though she never asked, and then she'd give me half back. One time I saved enough to buy a beautiful pair of brown boots. I liked clothes, even as a child and still do.

I usually got back by nine o'clock and there was always food on the table. My grandma made lovely soups and pies and scones and I used to love her apple and blackberry pie. After supper, I'd have a wash and a shave and, if my grandfather wasn't there to make me, my grandmother would. I'd heat up the water and wash in a bowl, always outside, even in winter. We had a canopy that was tied down and set behind the *vada* with barrels of hay round it to stop the draught. That's where we washed the clothes, too, and we had an old fold-up mangle to squeeze the water out.

In the end, I had to stop going on the knocker because there were a lot of robberies at that time. It was very difficult. People wouldn't open their doors and police used to supply them with 'No Hawkers' stickers.

Every year, we used to go to the Appleby Gypsy Fair in Cumbria and once my grandma said, 'You see that lady over there? She's your mother. Do you want to go and say hello?' I said, 'No, she ain't. You're my mother, I don't know that lady'. I wasn't bitter about what she'd done. It was just one of those things you couldn't change. And that was the end of it.

Many Romany children don't go to school as they're travelling most of the time. They speak their own Romany language and obviously a bit of English but most can't read or write. If parents want them to learn they can go to an Elder who would be able to teach them a little but they often say they are alright as they are. They can understand each other and why should they want to learn anything else? But times have changed.

One day, when we were parked at Banstead, I came home from work and my grandmother, who never worried about anything said, 'We've got a bit of a problem, boy.' I said, 'What's that?' 'Well, the school people have been round to this site and all the children who aren't going to school, have to go.' 'Well,' I said, 'that's ridiculous. They

8

might move on in three months time.' I'd been brought up with common sense. She said, 'Well, just to save any problems, will you go, just turn up?' I said, 'All right'.

It's very difficult for people to understand but when I was thirteen, I had a brain of a man of twenty-two and the same attitude. So to me, working on the streets was fine, but there was no way I could sit in a classroom with thirteen year-old children.

But I went to the school and found the headmaster. I said, 'Hello, I'm John Lee. I've got to come to school.' 'Ah yes,' he said, 'one of the gypsy people'. That got my back up straight away. Why should I be different from anyone else? Why did he have to say that? So I said, 'Yes, I'm one of the gypsy people'. He asked if I'd ever been to school before and I said no. 'Can you read or write?' 'I can't read, but I can add up.' 'Well, go into class seven'. There were boys in that class my age throwing bits of paper about. I thought, what am I doing here when I can make a living to put food on the table? Then the teacher walked in and before he started reading out the register, he said, 'We have a new pupil in today'. Well, everyone knew I was new. They'd never seen me before. He called out, 'John Lee'. I said, 'Here'. He looked at me and said, 'John Lee?' And I said, 'Yes, I'm here.' I thought he might be a bit deaf. So I stood up and said, 'That's me, I'm here' and sat down.

'Come out here,' he said. 'Are you talking to me?' I asked. 'Yes,' he said 'come out here'. I went, 'Just a moment. I was brought up to show respect to people. Respect is not given, it's earned.' The kids were all quiet. I said if he wanted me to show him respect, he'd got to earn it. 'I want you out here', he said. I thought right, do I give in or do I not? It's the first day, it's going to cause problems with my grandma, so I got up and walked up to him. I said, 'Don't ever talk to me like that again.' A thirteen year old kid to say that to a man! Kids don't talk like that, do they? He said, 'How old are you?' I told him. 'But, let me tell you before I go any further, I've got a mind of a man of twenty two or twenty three and an attitude to go with it. What I can see is that you and I are not going to get on. This is not the place for me, I sit in the street earning a living. This is a kindergarten. I was throwing paper like this when I was seven or eight. So the best thing before we have any more problems is for me to go home'. And I walked out. That was the end of my schooling. The other boys in the class were all giggling.

I would like to have learnt to read and write, but I didn't like his attitude. We would have been at loggerheads for ever and I wouldn't have learnt anything.

When I got home my grandmother asked how I got on and I said I wasn't going back there no more. She said, 'Well, forget it'. 'There's a big country out there, grandma,' I told her. 'We can go where we want, when we want. We don't have to be tied down to anything or anybody.' That was the end of my schooling.

My grandfather said, 'Well, I suppose it had to come to that really, you being what you are. That's the way I brought you up, to take care of yourself, but not to be rude to people.'

A few years later, when I was about sixteen, my grandparents sat me down and told me again that I was going to have a hard life. And I said, 'How, I've got an easy life?' My grandmother said, 'You're never going to be allowed to get married to a gypsy girl. You're not going to be able to live life as a gypsy, you're going to have to live as a *gorger* and you'll have to learn all about their way of life. It's completely different from ours'. They explained to me that it would be hard for me to change from one life to another, but that I would have to abide by their laws. I said, 'I'll worry about that when it happens. While you're alive, I'm staying with you.' And that's what I did.

But Romany gypsies are very different from other people and the most important thing for them is their blood line. It has to be absolutely pure. For hundreds of years they've travelled the countryside in rural areas, made camp, stayed a few days, then moved on. They seldom mix with anyone but their own and are so clean you'd never know they'd been there. Farmers like them as they're very hard-working and love working the land; they feel it's there to be looked after and taken care of, it's part of them. They're no trouble whatsoever and in winter and summer they always have somewhere to stay and work to do. But times have changed for them, more than for most people. It's much harder now, they can't travel like they used to with all the cars and traffic on the roads. At one time, there were lots of organised places where they could go and live, but not so many now. They still travel in their *vadas*, have horses and lurchers for hunting.

Romany men will always wear brown boots, and a brightly-coloured silk scarf in memory of dead gypsies. It has to be the best, an old nylon one wouldn't be good enough. But you're unlikely to meet a Romany gypsy because they usually keep themselves to themselves and stay in their own community unless they're working.

Children work on the land with their parents, pick peas and potatoes, help with the cooking. They are all taught a craft of some description: the girls learn to make dresses and pinafores; their clothes have to be clean every day and you can always see lines of washing hanging out to dry. They're taught to cook and make jewellery with stones and shells. And lavender bags. The boys work on the land, make clothes pegs, help with lambing, hedge cutting.

They all love listening to their grandmothers telling stories in the Romany language which are passed down the generations. You'd have to live amongst them to understand it. Sometimes, there's someone who plays the accordion or a fiddle or knocks on a kettle drum. Traditional Romany music, too, is passed down and often made up as the player goes along.

They buy very little orthodox medicine because they know how to use everything Mother Nature supplies. Dock leaves, for instance. These grow by railway lines and are good for bruises. If you've cut yourself, they'll put salt on it straight away, get a dock leaf and wrap it round the cut. They only go to hospital if it's urgent. If someone broke an arm, they'd use two bits of wood for splints to set it.

Chapter 3

I become a cruise ship waiter. The lady from
Argentina. My anti-apartheid row on a Cape Town
bus. I visit a banned black jazz club.

One day when I was seventeen, I was in a pub and got talking to a guy I'd known for some time. We both felt we'd like to go round the world. 'Why don't we join the Merchant Navy?' he said. 'How do you get in?' I asked. 'Oh, you go down to Southampton, go to the office and say you want to join'. So we did. We took some money and a few clothes and set off. The officer asked us how soon we wanted to start. 'You can go tomorrow on the *Braemar Castle* if you like, they're looking for stewards.' They gave us our uniforms but took the cost out of our wages and we went off to our cabins and the dining hall. It was enormous. It was morning and not busy and I was told which was my table and that I had two sittings of twelve people for lunch and dinner. We didn't have to wait at table at breakfast.

I couldn't read or write so I thought what do I do? There was a guy at the next table and he was putting the cutlery out. It was all silver service. I thought if I do what he's doing, I'll be all right, tables had to be the same. I was watching him and he caught me looking. He must have guessed what I was doing. 'You've never been a waiter in your life, have you?' he said. 'Who are you talking to?' I replied crossly. He said he was trying to help me. 'I know you've been watching me. I just made a mistake and you've done the same thing.' I admitted I'd never been a waiter and he said he'd help me out.

At dinner, everyone had a menu but the trouble was I couldn't read it. 'Dear oh Lord,' the other waiter said, 'how are you going to get on?' 'Well,' I said, 'I've got an idea. I'll just give them a pen and they can tick off what they want. Then I'll take the menu to the kitchen. I'll get by.'

They all came in, poshed up, in evening dress and sat down. My waiter friend had told me that I had to tell them my name and that I was going to be their waiter for the next nine weeks and if there was anything I could do for them, they should just ask me. Then, thinking of a way to get round not being able to read the menu, I said 'There seems to have been a few complaints lately about people not getting what they've ordered. So that there's no mistakes this time, I'm going to get you to tick off on the menu what you'd like.' Of course, I made all that up. Then I said, 'There are lots of soups, so hands up who wants soup.' Everyone laughed. The other waiter nearly fell through the floor

He called me over. 'You can't say 'hands up, who wants what?' he said. So I had to go round to each person and they had to tick off the soup they wanted. The first night was difficult because there was so much to learn. I used to take the menus to study in my cabin the evening before, and put numbers by the dishes. But I got used to it and they got used to me. They laughed about it and I never did tell them I couldn't read or write.

There was one quite large fellow and he couldn't easily get into his chair in the lounge area. One evening I said, 'Excuse me, sir, can I help you? I can get you a larger chair.' 'Would you?' he answered. I thought, I don't know how I'm going find one but when we weren't busy I went into the dining room and there was one there. The head waiter asked me what I was doing and I said someone had a bad leg and his chair wasn't right for him. He said, 'Oh, you're looking after him?' And I said, 'Of course I am.' 'Ok, then you carry on, that's fine.'

The food on the boat was very good. Sometimes I used to order an extra meal for one of the passengers and then take it back to my cabin. Nobody queried the number of plates you were asking for. There were twelve of us in the cabin and I'd walk in of a night time and they'd say, 'What you got there?' I'd give them a few bits and pieces. One night there were great big lobsters but I didn't know how to eat them! It was a long way to walk to the cabin with all those plates though I'd learnt how to carry them on my arm. At dinner, I used to think, I'll have that tonight and order an extra portion. I'd put them in one of the dumb waiters that weren't being used and then take it back to our cabin.

I went from the *Braemar Castle* to the *Edinburgh Castle* and did a couple of trips there. It was a hard boat to get to work on, everything was so good, sailors wanted to be on it. It was more sophisticated than the *Braemar* with millionaires and people like that. You had to clean the silver and glasses and three managers would go round the tables before the passengers arrived, to check them. I used to take mine to my cabin at night and get them ready for the morning. It was hard work. We had to get up at 6 o'clock and scrub the corridors, though you got extra money for that.

It was on the *Edinburgh Castle* that I met an Argentinian lady. The first night she came to the restaurant we were told not to pull the chairs back for passengers but to let them do it themselves. If you pulled one back and there was an accident, we'd be sued. I like nice women and I've never been slow in coming forward but I try not to make too many mistakes. This lady came into the restaurant and she looked absolutely beautiful. I said, 'Good evening'. She spoke English in a very seductive way, if you know what I mean. She never meant it like that but that was the way it was. She talked quietly and slowly and said, 'May I have....'? And I said, 'you can have anything you like.' She wanted a cocktail so I went and got it for her and we got quite chatty. There was a dance on the Friday night and this was Tuesday. The next day she asked me if I was going and would I accompany her? I told her we weren't allowed to. She said surely I could get there, couldn't I? Nobody would know.

15

I thought I'd take a chance. What could they do to me, throw me off the boat? I had a suit with me. One of the crew in the cabin asked me where I was going. I said just for a walk. In those days I never used to tell anybody anything. I kept myself to myself. So I put this suit on and crept out. If people have always seen you in your whites, they don't recognise you when you have a suit on. You look so different out of uniform and the crew in my cabin were so busy working they didn't really notice. We went to the dance, had a drink, and I finished up in her cabin. After that, I'd often go and mix in the bar with the first-class passengers and most of them thought I was one.

She got off at Quebec. She did give me her address, but I couldn't read it and I couldn't have given her mine because I never had one. The boat was my address. I never did get in touch with her.

It was when I was on the *Southern Cross* and half way to Australia that we had a strike. A union man on the boat said we had to stop work because they wouldn't give us a rise, though you could get better money on the boat than you could ashore. The boat was in the middle of the ocean and we were stranded for three days. The chefs were still cooking because they were in a different union but passengers had to help themselves. We only had two days in Australia and we weren't allowed to go ashore, you couldn't question this because they were the Captain's orders. Captains in those days had a lot of sway. They could even summon passengers up in front of them, if they thought they'd done something wrong.

I ended up waiting on the captain's table, what they called the Captain's Tiger, as his personal steward. I'm not a nervous person but before I accepted the position, I asked the head waiter what it was like? He said it was easier than what I'd been doing and there was more money and tips too. Of course I still couldn't read but I'd go over to each person at the table and remember what they'd said and what line it was on the menu. There was only the captain and maybe his six guests, so not a great big table like before when I had two sittings of twelve. But it was quite a lot to remember.

Normally, you had to stand back while passengers were eating but at the captain's table you had to stand near a passenger but out of earshot and watch to see if anyone had an empty glass. When that happened, you'd go over and pour the wine for them. I went right up to the top with the Captain's Table. I was No. 1 waiter. I'm not blowing my own trumpet but if I'm going to do something, I do it to the best of my capability. My table was always nice and clean, no dirty spots, everything was white. I was getting about £50 a month and then you had tips. The chap I got the chair for had given me £20.

Sometimes we'd anchor off shore and have three hours on land, maybe stay for one or two days. A few of the crew often got stranded – they'd fallen in love with a place and thought they'd live there. Once a couple of lads just missed the boat but knew they'd get another one when it came. They didn't let sailors off the boat at all in New Zealand. I think at that time a lot of people wanted to emigrate and thought this was a good way to get there for nothing. They'd get out there and never come back.

It was when we were in Cape Town that Jimmy Glass (another waiter) and I decided to jump ship. We were having such a good time there that we decided to stay, though when we first arrived we were shocked to see the way some black people lived. It was in holes in the ground – we couldn't believe it. They had no roofs and would cook down there and the children would just be running around in the streets.

One day, I caught a tram, went upstairs and the passengers were all black. I wanted to smoke and at that time in England you had to go on the top deck. I sat down next to this black fellow and the conductor came up and told me I couldn't sit there. I said, 'Why not?' He said that place was for black people. So I said to the man next to me, 'Excuse me, but you don't mind me sitting next to you, do you?' He turned away, didn't want to get involved.

I asked the conductor to explain why I couldn't sit there. 'Well you're English, and in England where do you sit?' I said, 'Anywhere there's an empty seat.' And he said, 'Not in South Africa. Black people sit upstairs, whites downstairs.' 'But I want to smoke a cigarette,' I replied. 'In England you only smoke upstairs.' 'Well here you can smoke downstairs'. I asked him why he was going to all this trouble and why didn't he just give me a ticket? I was only going a few stops. He wouldn't do it and I was adamant I wasn't going to move. I wasn't used to this apartheid nonsense. I said, 'I'm sitting where I am and if you don't want to give me a ticket, that's it.'

The tram stopped, the police came and I told them I'd never been in South Africa before. The policeman said there were lots of places black people couldn't go and I asked why? 'That's just the way it is,' he said. 'So if I wanted to go into a restaurant and it was full of black people, I wouldn't get served?' He said no, I wouldn't. So I got off the tram and walked; I didn't get a ticket.

I liked jazz and still do, Jelly Roll Morton was one of my favourites. I knew there was a terrific jazz club in Cape Town but I learnt it was for blacks only. We'd met two black guys and were talking about music and the jazz club and they told us that we wouldn't get in. Black people have their places, they told us, others have got theirs. I asked them if there was a whites' jazz club and they said, no, not in Cape Town. I thought, oh dear, because there was a pretty famous guy on in that club. Then they said, 'Well, look, we'll take you in there but you'll have to stand in the darkest corner you can find because if the police came I'd get a summons.' I said I'd just plead ignorance and that I didn't know, though apparently I would have been told on the door. I got in, and after that we used to go back every night with two girls we'd met there.

Being in Cape Town was an adventure, but being with black girls was illegal in the apartheid time. In the end, we decided it was time to leave. We went to the British

Embassy and they gave us the right documentation for getting work on the next ship leaving for the UK. It was the *Franconia,* a boat I'd worked on many times before.

It was back to being a steward, but after about three years I decided I'd got as far as I was going to, and thought I'd have a little rest.

Chapter 4

Life back home. My horses. The tailor in The Cut.
Grandfather and the pitchfork. West End jazz clubs. I
get married.

I was twenty when I came out of the Navy. I rented a small
flat in Battersea but I only stayed there a few days and
then went back to living in my *vada* on the site where my
grandparents were. My grandmother was not very well and
I wanted to be close to them. My grandfather bought me a
black stallion – I think he wanted to keep me at home. He
told me a horse was like a dog and if you wanted a dog to
be a friend, you got down to his level and talked to him,
then the fear of you standing over him is gone. It was the
same with a horse. 'You can't just stand in front of one
and put your hand on his head, because he can't see what
you're doing.' I loved riding that horse.

One day I discovered it had gone. I looked all round for
him but couldn't find him. Then my grandfather said he'd
taken him, someone had wanted to buy him. You couldn't
answer back. He'd made a decision. But he said he'd
bought me another one, better than Tom – we called them
all 'Tom', like dogs, I called them all dog – dog come
here, dog. It was a chestnut mare, a beautiful thing and he
told me I'd got to look after it. He got her out; it was
pouring with rain. I thought she was going to get soaked,
and covered her with a blanket from the tack room. My
grandfather came out and said, 'What you doing?' I said,
'She's getting soaking wet.' And he went, wallop, knocked
me on the ground. He said, 'Don't you dare cover her up.
Of course, she's wet, haven't you learnt anything yet?
Horses have got greasy skin and the water runs off. If you
cover her up, you're going to keep the damp in and she'll
get pneumonia. You only cover a horse before it gets wet,
not when it is wet. If it's wet it can't breathe.'

I've always saved money and I've always liked nice clothes. I knew a tailor called Hymie Harris down in The Cut at Waterloo and he was making me a suit for £15. I'd saved all my money for it. When you went in, he'd say, 'Ah boy, I've got a beautiful piece of material, why don't you have two suits and you can pay for the other one when you've got the money?' He'd make suits with what I call barrel back – all one piece of material, no joins in it, slightly tailored at the waist, then drop down. I bought this nice herring-bone suit. The other piece of material he had was a pearl grey barathea, it was so soft, lovely. I think if you had that suit made today, it would cost £500 to £600 or more.

One day I was going to meet a young lady. She was sixteen and I'd got suited and booted, a nice suit, brown boots, and was looking grand. My grandfather said, 'Where you going, boy?' I said, 'I'm going to meet someone'. 'A woman?' and I said, 'Yeah'. He said, 'Well, before you go, I want the tack room cleaned.' I went 'Now?' and he said, 'Yes, now. Change your clothes, it won't take you too long'. I said I'd be late. 'That's what I want done,' he repeated. 'I'll tell you what I'll do,' I offered. 'I'll get up extra early tomorrow morning and do it then.' He said he had some people coming to look at the horses and wanted it done now.

I looked at him. I'd never disobeyed him. But I said, 'No, I'm not doing it now.' It just came out of my mouth. He said, 'You are', and I said, 'I'm not. I told you I'll get up extra early in the morning and it will all be done before you get here.' I'd never spoken to him like that before. He said, 'You'll do it now' and got hold of this bull whip to flick me across the legs. It didn't mean anything, just enough to make me do what I was told.

So I picked up a pitch fork. He told me to put it down. I said, 'No'. 'What are you going to do with it?' he asked. I said I was defending myself. You could never frighten him. He said, 'Go on then, do what you want to do'. 'I don't want to do anything with it,' I told him. He was

21

challenging me because he knew I'd never get anywhere near him, he was too fast. I said, 'You put the whip down and I'll put the pitchfork down, and we can talk about it.' I was getting angry. So he rolled up the whip and put it down. I put the pitchfork down. He said, 'Come here'. I thought, no way, I'm not getting near an inch of him, he was too quick. I said 'No, we'll talk as we are'. He said 'I promise you I won't hit you'. His word was his bond. So I thought he's never lied to me before. I went over to him and he put his arms round me. 'I've been waiting two years for you to stand up to me', he said. 'I was testing you to see how far you'd go. You've gone all the way which is what I wanted you to do. If you don't want to do a thing, you don't do it. I'll buy you a shandy when you meet the young lady.' And he did.

The young lady wanted to marry me, but she was a bit possessive. I never dreamed about getting married because we were always travelling. You can't expect a *gorger* to do that. It might sound exciting, but it's not as exciting as it sounds. I was not courting her but I was taking her out, and she started talking about marriage. I didn't want to get married, I wanted to live life how I wanted to, though I didn't expect anyone to live the same way. 'It's no good crying,' I told her, 'you'll find someone better than me – I wouldn't be any good to you anyway. And that's the way it's got to be.' You didn't live with each other in them days, you didn't have a partner, you got married. That was it. But I thought that life wasn't for me. I was a wanderer.

At that time, I used to go up to West End jazz clubs five times a week and every Sunday night I'd go to the dance at the Lyceum. I was a good jiver. At the end of the evening, four or five of us from Battersea would go into Lyons Corner House which was quite near. There was a jazz club in Frith Street and sometimes I'd go to Ronnie Scott's. I liked big bands too, like Duke Ellington and Stan Kenton. They were all famous people at that time.

I remember meeting a young lady at the Lyceum and

we started dancing – she was a good jiver too. I asked her if I could take her home. She said, well, she lived a long way away in Barnet, and I said don't worry about that. But I missed the last tube home and trams didn't run at night. At two in the morning there was no transport, and buses only every hour. I thought I'd better start walking, just keeping to the main road. I saw a bus but it wouldn't stop. I walked all the way from High Barnet to Archway – a good ten miles – then caught the first bus into Chelsea. I couldn't read bus destinations but I could read their numbers – I'd seen numbers on coins when I was counting money for the chairs. I didn't see that young lady again.

One day, I was about twenty three, John Lee, one of the Elders on the site, came to me and told me his daughter, Ruth, hadn't got long to live but had always wanted a gypsy wedding. I'd always wanted one, too, but as I was only half gypsy I knew I wouldn't be able to have one. Ruth told me she didn't want me to do this for her but I said she was doing it for me. She could hardly walk, she was so frail and I used to go round and sit with her in her *vada*.

The traditions of gypsy weddings go back a long way. When a young couple fall in love, there's no such thing as an engagement. The man goes to the girl's family and tells the father they would like to get married. He (the father) tells him they must go and see the Elder who tells them they will be given a year's courtship and be chaperoned everywhere. Even if they go out for a walk, they must have one of the family with them. After a year, the couple go in front of the Gypsy Council and are asked how they are getting on. If all is well, the man is told he has to start putting money aside to buy a *vada* to live in. At the end of the second year, the Elder tells them they must make up their minds because once they are married they can never leave each other. After the third year they make a date for the wedding. The Elder will be there with his great book which lists all the marriages with names and dates. The couple don't live together until they are married and it's taboo for them to sleep together until then. But the two families do travel together for the young couple to get to know each other.

When they have decided to get married, they let their relations know and they all come to the piece of ground where they're staying and have what they call the *Wedding over the Broomsticks*. There was a bit of an uproar about our wedding. And of course we couldn't do it the traditional way.

But her father explained the situation to the others and told them there was no possibility of there being any children, so there was no blood line lost. 'John is giving my daughter something she's always wanted,' he told them.

So we got married and she got what she wanted and I got what I wanted too. We danced around a fire with five broomsticks, there was music and lots to eat: dishes of stewed rabbit, squirrel and hedgehog, which has a fishy taste. We used to eat off slates (now very popular in trendy restaurants), but then we had them because you could clean them, they didn't carry diseases. If a slate cracked, you just threw it away. For pudding, we had lots of pies: baked apple, apple and raspberry, cream and custard, with cider to drink.

One of the Elders wrote our names down in the large book which would be there for ever. Ruth went to her *vada* and I went to mine. She died a few months later in my arms. If a Romany gypsy has been married, he or she can never marry again, even if the other person dies. But there was no way I could have got married to a gypsy woman and had children, because I would have brought the same shame on them that my mother had put on me.

Chapter 5

My grandparents' death. I learn to drive trucks, a fire engine, an ambulance, a low level loader. I have a holiday in Spain.

My grandfather died in 1954 at ninety four when I was twenty four and my grandmother two years later at ninety six. I missed them a lot – they'd brought me up and I knew life would change. I respected my grandfather but I would have done anything for my grandmother. Her death knocked me 'bandy' in Romany language. She made me feel close to how I was brought up and her death broke my link with the past. I felt lost. For a while I didn't have any heart or soul to do anything. I had a Ford Cortina and for two years I slept in it and washed in streams and gentlemen's toilets in towns. I knew life would get harder but just didn't know what to do with myself and couldn't settle. I thought I wouldn't be able to stay on a gypsy camp – they wouldn't accept me because of my broken blood line. But I had some money in the bank and I went to find the Gypsy Council and asked them what I should do. They said, 'Well, you know you can't carry on living as a gypsy.' I said yes, I knew that. I still had my own *vada* They asked me what I was going to do with the horses and I told them I'd be taking them with me. I wasn't going to leave anything behind. They weren't nasty but that was it. I thought, well, if they didn't want me, I'd go on my own. I've always felt that when something difficult happened, I'd know how to handle it.

So I set off with the *vada* and the horses and went down into Battersea and then Banstead, because I knew some people there. But I was told I couldn't live there either. They didn't actually throw me off the site but told me that because my grandparents weren't alive any more I couldn't mix with gypsies. The funny part about it was that when my grandparents died the gypsies I was mixing with just turned like that and wouldn't have anything to do with me. The only reason they had allowed me to be there before was because of my grandparents. They didn't want me to get involved in anything and, as I couldn't marry one of the gypsy girls or have children, what good was I? That's the way they looked at it and that's the way they are. They are so loyal to their traditions, it's unbelievable. They would sooner have their hands cut off than go against them.

Of course, I could have stayed on the land my grandfather owned, but it had too many memories for me and I couldn't do that.

My grandmother always told me what would happen in the future. 'You're never going to be a proper gypsy, you're not going to be able to live the life you're living now, you're going to have a different one, go different ways. You can revert back to being a traveller and things like that, but you can't live as a gypsy on a gypsy site.' I told her I would be able to do anything I liked. If I didn't want to live in a house, I wouldn't.

So I thought well, if Romany gypsies didn't want me, I'd go on my own. It used to make me sad, but not now. I can understand that their blood line is the most important thing in their lives and they're brought up strictly because of that. They're never going to change and there's nothing I can do about it. I thought, if I've got to live like half a gypsy, I've got to get rid of the horses and get a car or a van and buy a proper caravan. And that's what I did. I went travelling in Hampshire and stayed on ordinary sites, but caravans weren't like they are now with electricity and all that. I had Calor gas and two ten-gallon milk churns that I'd fill with water at a garage and put on the back of the caravan. It was hard in the winter. Many sites were closed and I knew eventually I would have to go and live in a house.

Losing the horses was difficult, I'd had them a long time, but I kept the *vada* and still have it. One day I'd love to get a pair of horses and drive it from Sevenoaks to Tunbridge Wells where I live, because a horse and cart has the right of the road over everything. I could go in the bus lane and they couldn't stop me. I think you don't have to have a licence either and perhaps no insurance.

Out of curiosity I recently phoned a couple of insurance people and asked them, if I had a horse and cart, would I have to have insurance to put it on the road? They said they didn't know. I don't think they'd ever been asked that.

One evening, back in London, I met a fellow in Battersea called Charlie Hill. He had a big yard in Clapham and used to go to car and lorry sales. If there was an ambulance or a fire engine for sale, he'd get there first to buy it. One day he asked me if I could drive. I said I could but hadn't got a licence. He said I shouldn't worry about that, if I was driving a lorry that belonged to the owner who was a dealer, he had plates and they covered insurance. He asked me if I wanted a job and I said no, I didn't. Then he said could I do him a favour? I said, 'Yeah, I'll do you a favour, what is it?' 'Can you take this ambulance down to such and such a place and I'll give you a day's money?' I agreed. Then I had to take a fire engine down to Southampton Docks and show the buyer how to work the pump. Charlie handed me the keys and showed me what to do. I drove it down and when I arrived I saw the bloke and showed him how to how to connect the pump to the main water supply, switch it on and turn a handle. I showed him all this and he said, 'But there's no water in it.' And I said of course there wasn't, you had to fix it to the mains and the water would come shooting out. Push that button, pull that lever, put your hose on the end of it and have the water running through. He understood it in the end.

The worse moment I had was driving a 60ft-long Scammell low loader to Frimley where there was a big car sale. It was a big long lorry with a trailer on the back I never say no to anything unless it's the wrong side of the law or detrimental to me, so I went over to Charlie's yard and there was this big lorry and trailer. The mechanic told me it had no accelerator pedal and the only way I could drive it was with a strong piece of wire to use instead. He said he'd put a wooden handle on it so I could use it by hand instead of by foot. I said, 'Well fit it up and let's have a go.' I drove it round the yard. It was a bit funny at first. You wanted to push your foot down. But I got used to it. I said I could handle it but he said I shouldn't forget I hadn't got the trailer on the back. I thought, well, the trailer has only got to be judged by length going round roundabouts, it has nothing to do with the engine. So I took it down to Frimley but it never sold and I had to bring it back.

One day, I asked myself what was I doing all this for. I suppose I'd been working for Charlie Hill for about three years on and off, driving all sorts of vehicles. I thought I'd have a little holiday.

Even though I couldn't read I never had any trouble getting around in other countries, on planes or in restaurants. I could always make myself understood. I went away for two weeks and stayed three months. It was in Magaluf, in Mallorca, which has a bad name now, but it didn't then, there was only one hotel there. I was on the beach one day soon after I'd arrived, and a man came along selling watches. I spoke a little Spanish and told him to go away and I didn't need any. He spoke a bit of English and I decided to ask him if he knew a nice bar to have a drink of an evening. He said they all drank in one down the road and I thought I might go there that night. I got suitably booted and went down to the bar. One of the musicians came over and talked to me and we had a good drink that night. My friend from the beach told me there was a party on Saturday and asked if I'd like to come? I went and met his sister who was a flamenco dancer. A beautiful dancer. I got mixed up with her. I didn't fall in love but I liked her. But time was running out and so was my money. As I couldn't write, I asked her to send a telegram to John Lee, the Elder, whose daughter, Ruth, I'd married, saying, 'In trouble, send more money'. He sent me quite a lot and I stayed and went to the flamenco clubs with her.

A year later I was back in Battersea, running my own building business.

Chapter 6

I start a building company. I teach a blind orphan girl in Malta to cane chairs.

I'd seen a nice ground floor flat advertised in Bennerley Road, Battersea, with an old couple living upstairs. It had a sitting room, dining room, kitchen and garden at the back. I thought that would suit me. It was the 1960s and easy to find a flat in those days. But the old couple above had to pass my sitting room to go upstairs. I wasn't very happy with this so I went to the estate agent and asked if they could make the door smaller there would be room to make a little passage from the front door to the stairs. OK, he said, he'd think about it.

It was a Victorian house and had beautiful plastered ceilings with roses. I had painted my rooms, picking all the roses out in colours and the agent said he thought I'd made a good job of it. He asked me if I was a builder and I said I wasn't. He asked me if I'd like to do some decorating work for him and I said yes, sure. He asked me if I was capable of changing the doorway in the hall and I said I could. So I made my door smaller, put in a partition wall to give me more privacy and everything was all right.

This gave me the idea of starting my own business and I called it Croy Builders – I saw the name in a magazine. The first job I did was a greengrocer's shop and I went round with the estate agent to see it. There were three floors which had to be turned into flats. The agent asked me if I thought I could handle it? I said, 'No problem.' If I couldn't do it, I could always find someone who could. It meant knocking down a partition wall, putting in a staircase and a passageway. I found a plumber to put bathrooms and toilets in, electricians and plasterers – they were all self-employed. I paid them money and put my little bit of profit on top. After that the agent gave me another job: to convert a shop into a hairdresser's. We had to take the shop down and build it up on the pavement which meant getting a holding licence. There was an architect from Wandsworth Borough Council there and one day he asked me if I had plenty of work. And I said, 'Yes.' 'You want any more?' He ended up joining my company. I'd started it off from nothing and ended up, four years later, with twenty two people – carpenters, plumbers, and bricklayers – working for me.

But then the building trade went into a recession. The agent went out of business and emigrated to New Zealand with his family. I sold Croy Builders after four years for good money.

Before going back to caning chairs, I went to Malta for a little holiday. One day I was looking round one of the churches – I've always been interested in carving work – and a bloke came up and asked if he could help me. Maybe you'd be interested in seeing our children, he said. I discovered there was a school attached to the church for orphans from about nine to thirteen years old and some of them were blind.

I walked in and there was this little girl, about thirteen, who was putting cane on a chair. The teacher said she was going to try and make a pattern. I said I did that for a living. He said, 'You don't, do you?' I went over to have a word with her. She was feeling the cane and weaving it in and out. It was straight as a die. She counted the holes and found out where to put the cane. I asked the teacher how she knew to keep the cane in such a straight line. The teacher said she had a picture of what she wanted in her mind.

The girl spoke a little English and the teacher translated. She told me how she did it, touching the cane and feeling where it went. I offered to help her. The teacher asked if I was on holiday and I said I was there for a couple of weeks. 'If I gave you accommodation,' he said, 'would you come up here to help us for a few months?' I stayed about six and used to go up every day. I was with that little girl most of the time, but the others got interested too. I got to know her very well and she became very good.

They gave me a party before I left and thanked me. She was a lovely kid. I had this thing in my head that I would like to adopt her. I really would like to have looked after her. But I didn't feel I knew enough about children, and with the life I led and my Romany traditions, it might not have worked. I'll never know.

During this time I'd had a break from chairs, and now I thought I'd go back to them. My grandmother had told me they would always be a way to make a living and I was getting more orders than ever. I'd never been so busy and I met some interesting people in the area. I did a couple of chairs for David Frost. He said he didn't want me to take them out into the street because they were valuable. I said that was fair enough, I could do them inside. I worked there for two days and he never offered me a cup of tea! The funniest person I met was Dave Allen, the comedian. He was a right good fellow. I did a couple of chairs for him and we'd finish up in the pub.

Chapter 7

Meeting Jennifer. I go to the opera.

One day in 1964, I was sitting in the King's Road, Chelsea caning chairs, when a Rolls Royce pulled up and the driver went *toot toot* and beckoned me over. Not in a million years, I thought. If you want me, you come to me. He tooted twice but I took no notice. I called out to him to come over. He got out of the car and walked over, slamming the car door. You never slam doors on a Rolls Royce or any beautiful car – they just shut themselves. 'Madam has two chairs she'd like caned,' he said. 'Well, put madam's name, phone number and address in my book,' I told him. The book is for customers to give me their details and I can contact them later. I still couldn't read and had to work out where she lived by taking individual letters of her address on the street map. I thought, well, that's a posh address. It was on the Embankment near the Chelsea Pensioners' homes.

I went round to see her. Inside the building I could see a porter sitting in an office. I rang the bell and he opened the front door. 'Yes,' he said 'what do you want?' I said I'd come to see Mrs. Stableton and he said, 'No, not here mate, we don't have tradespeople.' I said, 'Just a minute, I've come to see Mrs. Stableton.' 'Have you got her flat number?' 'Yes, Flat 2'. 'Hold on a minute, who are you?' I said I was the chair caner. He rang through and said he had a chair caner with him. And she said to send him through. The porter told me to go over there, open two doors and stand there. 'When one door shuts I'll open the other one. She's the first flat on the left.' So I went in.

A little maid came to the door. I told her I'd come to see Mrs. Stableton. 'Oh, she's in bed,' she said. I said I'd come back later. 'Oh no, no, no, she's had a bit of an accident and we had to bring the bed from downstairs to upstairs.' It was a weird flat. The bedrooms were all downstairs. A little voice called out, 'Hello.' The maid said, 'She wants to see you.' So I went in and there she was lying in bed, she'd busted her ankle. She told the little maid there were two chairs downstairs, and would she bring them up? I said I could mend them and told her my address. I wanted her to have that.

She didn't have any make-up on but she had had her hair done. She was about forty four, ten years older than me at the time. By the time I'd done the chairs, she was out of bed. I don't know if that porter had taken an instant dislike to me. I never said anything rude to him but he seemed to get a little bit over the top possessive. 'That's beautiful work,' Mrs. Stableton said when I brought them back. 'I'm sorry I haven't got any more chairs for you to do, but could you paint a door for me?' I said, 'Yeah, I can paint a door.' Anybody can paint a door. She said she'd had builders in and they'd extended a room, and put a new door in the frame, but hadn't come back to paint it.

We went to look at the door. 'I can do that,' I said. She never asked how much things cost. 'When could you start?' I knew a painter and went over to ask his advice. He said if it was new wood you had to put knotting oil on the knots or they'd bleed. 'Let it dry, sandpaper it down, put on two undercoats and give it at least a week to dry. Then you start glossing it.' He said he'd give me a couple of nice brushes. I said I'd buy them off him – that's the way I am. I believe in fair play. He asked me how much I was charging and that it shouldn't be less than £25. I thought that was a lot of money. He said that's what he'd charge and he didn't want me doing it for less.

I painted the door and as I was leaving Mrs. Stableton asked me if I'd like to go to the opera that Friday. Well, I've always been game to do anything but I didn't know what opera was. A picture palace? So I said yes, I'd like to go. She said could I be there at 5.30p.m.?

On the way home I thought, what have I got myself into? What is this opera business? I had a friend who worked in a solicitor's office and I thought I'd go and ask him. I said I'd come for some advice and he said, 'You're not in trouble are you?' I said, 'You know me, I don't get into trouble.' I said I was going to the opera on Friday. He nearly fell off his chair. He said he hadn't got time for messing about, what did I want? I said I was going to the opera on Friday evening. He said, 'Oh, one of those concerts in a village hall,' and I said, 'No, it's Covent Garden.' He said 'Covent Garden, you?' He thought I was pulling his leg. He asked whom I was going with and I said a lady.

I asked him what opera was, and what I had to wear? I had suits because I used to have them made down in the The Cut. 'Do you know whether she's got a box or not?' he asked. I said I didn't know anything about it, but what was it?

'It's not a picture palace,' he said, 'and I don't know whether you'll like it but it's all in Italian.' It was a chance in a life time and I should definitely go. 'If you don't like it, sit there and suffer because there's not many people of our class who go to the opera. It's for High Society and very expensive.'

I wanted to know what I had to wear. 'Well, is she a Lady?' he asked. I said I didn't know, but that she talked very posh. Where did she live? I told him. He said, 'Well, she'll either have a box and if she hasn't got that, she won't be sitting any further back than three rows from the front. You'll have to wear evening dress.' I said: 'What? Them frilly shirts and bow ties? I can't wear stuff like that.' He said, 'That's what you've got to wear. Be sensible, you'll never have a chance like this again. Go to Moss Brothers, tell them what you're going to do and they'll fit you out.' So I go there and they give me all this stuff.

I have a hair cut and try the suit on. Well, I couldn't get it off quick enough – I looked like a pansy. Then I thought, if that's what it's got to be, that's what it's got to be. And if I didn't dress like that, they wouldn't let me in. It's not like going to a picture palace, it's different altogether.

It was in October and I left my dirty old van a couple of streets away. The porter didn't recognise me. He said: 'Good evening sir, I'll ring through to Mrs. Stableton.' He said, 'There's a gentleman here', and she said, 'Oh yes, that's all right I'm expecting someone'.

'My God, Jonathan', (that was the first time she called me Jonathan), 'you look very elegant. Come in.' She looked gorgeous. She'd had her hair done, it was on top with ringlets dropping down, rather an old fashioned look. Her dress was cut square across the top and she had a fox-fur stole and long gloves. The dress was pink, not pink pink, a sort of subtle colour between red and pink. I thought I don't know what I'm doing this for. Where am I going?

She asked me where my top coat was. Top coat, I thought, what's that? I said I hadn't got one. 'Oh, you'll have to have one', she said. 'Come with me'. So we went downstairs. She took a key, opened a door and the room was full of fitted wardrobes. She opened one – it was all men's clothes. She saw my face look a bit questioning. 'I can see you're wondering why all these clothes are here,' she said. But I told her it was none of my business, which it wasn't. 'They're my ex-husband's,' she explained. 'I haven't had the heart to give them to charity but I will one day. I'm going to find you a top coat.'

She brought out a beautiful overcoat with velvet round the collar and cuffs and it fitted me to a T. 'Now,' she said, 'we'll have to find you a white silk scarf. Have you ever worn one of these before?' I said not like that. 'You just put it round your neck and leave it where it lands.' I was beginning to think we must be going somewhere really important to be wearing all these clothes. 'We'd better be making a move,' she said. 'Here's the chauffeur you saw in the first place.' He never recognised me. 'Good evening, sir, good evening madam.'

So we get to Covent Garden and there was a guy, must have been the manager, who came running down the stairs to meet us. 'I've got everything you asked for,' he told her, 'a table in the restaurant and one in the bar during the interval.' I thought restaurant, restaurant, I ain't got money for a restaurant. I told myself that I'd always handled things when they came up against me one way or another and I didn't have to go to the restaurant. But I always tell people the truth and I'd have to tell her I'd not got any money for that.

We were sitting in the third row from the front and as she was going to sit down, someone in a box waved to her and she waved back, just like the Queen. She told me she'd let those people have her box for the evening because there were quite a few of them. Well, I thought, my friend was right. We sat down. I'd got my programme. She'd got hers. Of course, she didn't know I couldn't read. I thought I'd do what she was doing but not so fast. I was looking at her out of the side of my eye, and when she turned the page, I waited a bit, and then turned mine I didn't have a clue what I was doing but thought, well, just act it out.

Then she said, 'When you've read the synopsis of the first act, you'll get an idea of what it's all about.' 'Well,' I told her, 'as I've never been to an opera before could you explain a little bit?' I had to wriggle out of it somehow. She told me it was called *La Traviata*. 'Yes, I know that,' I said. 'It says that here,' and I pointed to the wrong word. She said it was with Joan Sutherland and that I couldn't have had a better introduction to opera than with her. The story was quite sad and when I looked at Mrs. Stableton she was wiping tears away. I really enjoyed it because even though I didn't know what it was about and didn't understand the language, I could understand their actions and their body movements.

In the interval, we went to a little round table in the bar where there were sandwiches and I thought all I wanted was half a lager with a little drop of lime. Jennifer (I was now calling her Jennifer) said would I excuse her a moment and she went over to the bar and told the barman 'to give the gentleman anything he wants and put it on my account'. I've got good hearing. When the barman came to the table, I said I'd like half a lager with a drop of lime. I think he'd never been asked for that before. I mean, you don't ask for half a lager at Covent Garden, do you? You have to have champagne or something like that.'

Jennifer had gone upstairs to talk with the manager and was away quite a long time. I was anxious about not having enough money to pay for a meal in the restaurant and thought I might be having to leave shortly and get home the best way I could. My grandpa always told me two things you never wait for: a bus or a woman.

When the opera was over, we went to the restaurant and I had a little sip of champagne, but didn't really like it. Joan Sutherland came up and kissed her. I didn't realise who she was and thought she must be a friend.

Then it was all over and the chauffeur took us home. I said goodnight. Then she asked if I'd like a coffee? I said I would. I thought I'd better go in or the chauffeur would think it rather odd. 'We must go to the opera again sometime,' she said.' I replied 'Yes, I'd like that' but thought, I've got to think about this – I'm not sure whether I like it or not. Then she said, 'Before you go, what are you doing on Tuesday?' I said working like I do every day. 'On Tuesday evening?' I said I hadn't got anything planned. Would I escort her to a restaurant? I said, 'What do you mean, take you to a restaurant, or what?' She said she was going to one but couldn't go on her own. I thought that's a bit weird. She said that when she went out, she'd phone up an agency and they'd send round an escort. 'But I don't know who I'm going to get. They are always polite but their interests might be different to mine.'

I said she didn't know me and she said, 'No, but you're interesting.' I didn't think I was. I asked where the restaurant was. It was a little Italian place in Ebury Street and there would be about twenty-six people. 'Friends of yours?' I asked. And she said mainly, yes. 'You mean you want me to be your escort?' And she said, 'Yes'. 'Well, I'm not anybody's escort,' I told her. 'I'm so sorry', she said. 'I understand what it must sound like. You're not my escort, you're my friend. Would you please escort me to the restaurant as a friend?' I said, 'That's better.' I don't know why I jumped at that particularly. I think I felt she was just going to use me. 'Do you think that would be possible?' she asked. She was a good looking woman. So I said, 'Yeah, OK, I'll go with you but I'm not wearing....' 'No,' she said 'it's not evening dress.'

'While we're in the restaurant,' she told me, 'we won't be sitting next to each other . It's man, woman, man, woman, and you don't know who you'll be next to. But if I need you during the dinner and I nod at you, will you go and stand at the bar?' I said yes, I'd do that.

I sat next to this woman, she must have been eighty, she was charming, but a foreigner. I tried to be as nice as I possibly could to make conversation with her. Then towards the end of the evening Jennifer nodded at me and I went to the bar. She asked me if I'd got some money on me. I said I'd got a few pounds and she said would I discreetly call the waiter and give him £10? I said, 'Don't worry about it, of course I will.' In a little while I nodded at the waiter and he came round. I said, 'This is for you.' He said, 'Thank you, sir'. He didn't put it in his pocket, he held it in his hand. Nobody knew what was going on. If he'd put it in his pocket, everyone would have realised it was a tip.

There was this Becher's Brook man there. I always called him Billy Becher because he reminded me of people in the racing fraternity. Loud mouthed he was. I could take him in small doses because I could see through him. During the meal I heard him say to Jennifer, loud enough for me to hear, 'Your Jonathan hasn't got a lot to say for himself.' And Jennifer said, 'No, but he thinks a lot.' And I thought well, that's nice. That's a good defence. For nearly twenty-five years after that, she always defended me.

At the end of the evening, everyone said goodnight. They were her friends, not her husband's. She'd been divorced for two years and had enough money to buy what she wanted. But she never flaunted it. That's what I liked about her. They'd had a big house in Hampshire and one weekend she went to see her mother who wasn't well. She was supposed to be going away for the whole weekend but came back the next day and found her husband in bed with two other fellas. That was the end of that marriage.

Chapter 8

Life with Jennifer. I learn to read and write. I go to a ladies' dinner party

Meeting Jennifer completely changed my life. About six months after we met and we'd been to the opera two or three times, she asked me if I'd move in with her. I said no. I told her I liked my own space and that I did things she might not like. I think she was lonely. She was in her mid forties and I was mid thirties. Even though she had the maid, she was in that flat all on her own. She'd get a couple of friends round, but all they wanted was to go out for a drink or a meal and she didn't want that. She wanted a man with her. As simple as that. She'd been married three times but none of her husbands were any good.

I was a very different kind of person. I was attentive to her. She might go to empty the rubbish bin, for instance, and I'd say, leave it, I'll do it. Her husbands would never have done that. She told me they'd say get the maid to do it. I used to help wash up even though she had a machine. I never lived with her but I had my flat in Battersea and I'd go over at week-ends.

It was about a month after our first opera and we'd been to three more, that I said I had a confession to make. I realised afterwards that word 'confession' was a bit of a stab in the back. Her three husbands had all gone off with other women except one who had gone with a man. She said was it serious? And I said no, not really. Just that I couldn't read or write. She couldn't believe it. She said, 'How did you get on when we went to the opera? I thought you could read.' I said I could recognise a few words, my grandmother was Italian. She said how had I managed, how had I found all the customers' addresses where I had to go to pick up the chairs?

I admitted it had taken me a couple of hours a night,

41

looking at the names, letter by letter and finding them on the map. But, once I go to a place, I can always find it again. When I was working in Chelsea, I knew where all the streets were like the back of my hand and probably knew the area better than people who lived there.

Jennifer said I couldn't go through life not able to read and write. I said I had so far. 'But it would be a lot easier if you could, wouldn't it,' she asked ? I admitted I couldn't even write my name. She got me a private tutor, a friend of hers, and told him about me, that she wanted him to teach me and she'd pay whatever it cost. So I went round to his house with other kids. Moneyed families they were. I didn't care about being with younger people and I've never been embarrassed in my life or been shy but I did ask myself what did I want to do this for? But once I started putting words together, I thought, well, this is interesting and because it was, I could get on with it. The teacher said to me after a year that if I'd had an education I'd have been a great pupil. I went for two years, three nights a week and began reading books. Jennifer helped me a lot, telling me how to pronounce a word. She was a lovely person.

We used to play chess, dominoes and Scrabble together. I think that was when my manners improved a great deal. I knew what you were supposed to do but I never used to do it. For instance, you don't hold a woman's arm, you hold her elbow. You don't put your arm round her waist. You open the door, but when you push it open, do you go in first and hold it open for her, or do you open the door and let her go first? I always walk on the kerb side.

One evening the doorbell rang and I thought it was my wholesaler sending me a parcel but it was Jehovah's Witnesses. I haven't got anything against anyone, and I'm not a particularly religious person but I sometimes think that if educated people believe in it, there must be something it. I just can't get my head round it. I told the Jehovah's Witnesses that I had one question to ask: what would happen if the Queen was an atheist? They said they'd never been asked that question and they didn't know the answer.

When we'd been together for about a year, Jennifer decided to have a dinner party in her flat. She told me it was for two reasons: one to celebrate us being together and the other because her friends were whispering about us and she thought she'd straighten it out. Some of the friends I'd met, some I hadn't. They were all women. I was the only fella there. They all came in, good evening, good evening and all that. Then before the meal was placed on the table, Jennifer gave a little speech. She'd asked me first if I'd mind and I said she must do as she wanted. First of all she said to everyone, 'Some of you know Jonathan, some of you don't, so I'm going to introduce him.' I stood there like a wally. I don't like being up front. I like to be on my own, out of the way.

She said she'd heard a little whisper going around about Jonathan and herself so she was going to explain what it was all about. 'Jonathan is a Romany gypsy,' she told them, 'and you will see him sitting in the King's Road caning chairs, which is what he does. He is my beau and my lover, he looks after me very well and we get on extremely well. This little party is for our year together.' She told them she had to say this because she didn't like people whispering behind her back.

Those who hadn't met me were quite surprised. I could see the look on their faces but she put it in such a way that they couldn't have disapproved even though some of them were a bit toffee-nosed and I don't usually get on with people like that. Not really and truly.

After Jennifer had given her little talk, some of them wanted to know this and that about my life, what it was like to be a Romany gypsy, what did they do? I said, well, it was difficult to explain, but the way Romany Gypsies lead their lives was completely different to the way they lead theirs. I explained a few things, but I don't like to be the centre of attention.

43

We were together nearly twenty five years, but we weren't tied at the hip. She asked me to marry her a couple of times but could you imagine if I'd done so, the problems there would have been, my goodness. I used to say, 'Why do we have to spoil it? Why can't we keep things as they are? I'll always look after you, take care of you, make sure everything is all right?'

She said, 'Oh well, if that's your decision' and looked a bit down in the dumps. I said it just wouldn't be possible for me to marry her. It would completely change my life and what would her family think? She had two grown-up children. She said she wasn't worried about them and I said I wasn't either but we were all right and happy as we were. And that was the way it was.

Sometimes I'd ask her why she was looking miserable and what was the matter, had she got a problem? 'Tell me,' I said, 'we might be able to change things.' She used to worry a lot and I'd say, 'What are you worrying about? If you can't change something, it's not even worth thinking about. Forget it.' 'It's not that easy,' she'd say. She said a lot of people couldn't do things like that, but it's common sense, isn't it? I was brought up on common sense and old sayings.

Chapter 9

Family affairs. Jewellery from the bank. Boating in Hampshire. A family wedding.

After we'd been together a few years, Jennifer decided she didn't want to go to society affairs any more. She just wanted to go out with me. She'd got fed up with them all, she said. They were false, just for show. She'd once had a large house in Hampshire and liked going on the river there. She'd hire a long boat and someone to drive it. I'd driven buses and trams, fire engines and all that, but never one of those boats, though I suppose it wasn't that difficult. The driver used to take us wherever we wanted to go up and down the river, sometimes for a week. It was nice.

One day I went to her flat, I had the key and the porter knew who I was by then. There were two men in business suits outside the front door. I thought, 'What's going on here?' I asked Jennifer who those two blokes outside were, was something wrong? 'Oh no,' she said, 'they were from the bank.' I asked what they were doing? She told me her daughter, Charlotte, was getting married and she'd had all her jewellery brought from the bank for her to choose something. On the table there was a green baize cloth with the jewellery on it, tiaras, drop earrings, bracelets, rings. God knows what they were worth. Charlotte was coming over that evening and going to pick out what she wanted for a wedding present. I'd only seen her once, never spoken to her.

She had the key to the flat and ran into the room. She never said, 'hello' to me, just to her mother. 'I'll have that, that and that', she said and laughed. Jennifer said she could have one piece only. She picked the tiara and a necklace. Jennifer said, 'No, only one piece.' Charlotte threw a bit of a tantrum. But they boxed it up and the blokes took the rest back to the bank. Charlotte never kissed her mother or said thank you. She just called out, 'I'm going now, Mummy. I'll see you at the wedding.'

I said to Charlotte, 'Give me that front door key. You don't walk in and out of here as you please.' She appealed to her mother but Jennifer said, 'Do what he says, give him the key.' Charlotte said she'd never been told what to do like that and slammed the door behind her. Jennifer said it was her father. He'd spoilt her terribly; she was never checked. I said if she was my daughter, I'd put her across my knee and slap her backside so hard she wouldn't be able to sit down for months. She was so rude. And Jennifer said, 'Yes, I know.' I asked if she wanted me to take her to the wedding? And she said, well, she wouldn't like to go on her own.

One day before the wedding her son came in and I took the key off him too. He was a big man and he'd had a lot of money from Jennifer to start businesses that were never successful. He was just a playboy; he had no idea about life.

The wedding was in three weeks time. 'Shall we have the chauffeur?' Jennifer asked. I said she must choose what she'd like to do, and she said she thought it might be best.

We went to the church. It was a nice wedding, but I didn't want to be introduced to her ex-husband. 'You and me, we're all right,' I told Jennifer, 'but that's it.' At the reception she said she'd have to leave me for a while and I said that was fine and I'd have a glass of wine and a cigar.

I was smoking the cigar, they were all smoking cigars and her son was with two friends. All of a sudden, I heard the word gypsy. I thought they're talking about me. And then I thought, forget it. But they started laughing and I thought that's it. I went over to them and said to her son, 'You and me, outside on the balcony'. He said, 'pardon?' And I said, 'Come outside on the balcony now.' He followed me out and I shut the door. I said, 'If I ever hear you talking about me again, belittling me in front of your friends, I'll break every bone in your body. What me and your mother do has nothing to do with you. She's old enough to do what she wants.' I said I'd got good ears and could hear what he was saying so he'd better go inside before I really got upset. I knew he was saying to his friends, 'That's my mother's boyfriend, he's a gypsy.'

I went over to his friends. I said, 'See you two, I can be a nasty person when I'm angry, don't ever discuss me and your friend's mother in my presence. I know what you were saying and it's got nothing to do with you. I'm not like anybody you know,' and I walked away. I was fuming.

Jennifer came in and said she was sorry she'd left me so long. 'You don't look happy,' she said. 'I'm not happy. I've just had to pull your son out on the balcony and threatened to break his arms and legs'. She laughed and said it was about time somebody did that.

Chapter 10

I start a vegetable stall. Covent Garden market. I cook beetroots, sell spinach. I open seven greengrocer shops.

About this time, I was thirty-seven, I thought I'd start a new business. I knew some greengrocers and decided to go into that. I opened a veg stall in the market in Northcote Road, Battersea, and a year later a small fruit and veg shop in Webbs Road also in Battersea. But there was only a little pavement by the shop so I made a shelf that I could drop down with boxes of stuff laid on them so people could see exactly what there was. Onions, bags of carrots, Brussel sprouts all hanging up on the walls.

It was very hard work. I'd go up to Covent Garden at three o'clock every morning and in the beginning I'd watch people and ask questions. I had to be back at the shop with the stuff by eight. I found out who the good wholesalers were and got a lot of my veg from Beesons, they were the best firm there and they'd give me a little bit of a discount and things like that.

I had the stall and shop for over a year and they were doing well. When I was getting really busy, the wholesalers would ask if I had a couple of shops as I bought so much stuff, and I'd say, no just one And they said, 'You're buying all that?' And I'd say I'd be back in two days time for more.

In the end I had a guy running the stall for me. I used to have a four-ton lorry to get all the stuff there. At that time there were a lot of black people in Battersea and I knew they liked spinach but nobody else sold it. So I went to market one day and there were fifty cases of spinach with no one wanting to touch them. I said to the wholesaler, 'I'll tell you what, I'll have the fifty boxes off you, and I'll give you eight pence a box for them.' He said, 'Come on, you've got to do better than that.' I thought well, that was rather little, so I said I'd give him ten pence a box and take the fifty. Which I did.

I asked the boy running my stall if he'd ever sold spinach and did he know how to wrap it up? He said no. I told him I'd come down the next day with fifty boxes and that he had to sell them all. I told him how to weigh it, then when it came to what the person wanted, wrap it up in newspaper. I priced it at fifteen pence a pound. In two days he'd sold the fifty boxes. People were buying it like lunatics, nobody else was selling it. I went back to Beesons, the wholesalers, and asked them how many boxes they'd got? I knew that if you didn't disturb spinach, it would last about a week in a cool place. 'Well,' he said, 'there's seventy boxes there.' I said I'd pay forty pence a box. 'What are you doing with all this spinach, not eating it, are you?' he asked. 'I don't know anyone else selling spinach like that.'

I used to cook my own beetroots, I loved the smell. They'd come out hot and I'd lay them on cabbage leaves to make them look nice. I'd display bunches of grapes with tomatoes, to make them look appetizing. I used to put bunches of asparagus standing upright in a saucepan, to show customers how to cook them. I had two big baths filled with water for the cabbages and in the summer I'd buy boxes of lettuces which were sometimes shrivelled up. I'd put them in the bath, leave them there, then hang them up and they'd get nice and crisp. I've not seen a Manchester cos lettuce for years. They were grown in black soil in Manchester and were absolutely beautiful. Sweeter than ordinary cos lettuces. They used to come with their stalks on and all the black earth. I don't think they grow them any more.

Food was very different then. It was fresh – today you don't know how long it's been in a fridge. I don't go into supermarkets if I can help it, but recently I wanted some potatoes and thought I'd pop into Morrisons on my way home. I picked up a bag of potatoes with a sell-by date on it. Sell-by date on potatoes? That's not necessary. I thought it must be a mistake and asked an assistant. He didn't know why it had that on it, so I asked to see the manager. 'Why is there a sell-by date on these potatoes? Was it a mistake?' I asked him. He went no, no. I said, 'You don't have to have that. What it should say is that they are not new potatoes, they are last season's.'

I asked him if he knew anything about veg. 'Well, no,' he said. 'Well, I'll tell you. Years ago, we used to have what they called clamps at the bottom of a field and a trench. You'd cover the trench with straw, pack the dug-up potatoes in it and that would stop them from sprouting for three or four months. The frost never got at them. Parsnips, turnips, they'd keep them all that way.' He said well, he never knew that and how did I know? I said I'd show him how to tell new potatoes from last year's crop. You just scrape off the skin with your thumb. If the skin doesn't come off, they're last year's.' 'Do you want a job here?' he asked. 'No, thanks', I said.

After a year, the shop and stall were doing very well, so I thought I'd expand. I exchanged the stall in Battersea for a small shop in Brixton. Fifteen years later, and a lot of hard work, I had shops in Streatham, Brixton, Battersea, Shepherd's Bush, Holland Park, Fulham, and a head office and shop in King's Road, Chelsea.

Chapter 11

My seven shops. King's Road dinner parties. Lloyd's of London crash.

Running all those seven shops was very hard work. I had to get to the market by 3am so hardly had any sleep. I had managers in each of them but I never had a business partner. It wasn't that I didn't trust people, just that I knew what I was doing and had a different way of doing things from others.

My best shop was in Western Avenue, Shepherds Bush. There were housing estates nearby and already two greengrocers. One came up for sale – it wasn't a lot of money and I thought what could I lose? I always had the other shops. So I bought it, it was a cut-price thing. The guy who had had it was a non tryer, but I'm a tryer. One day I bought a load of cauliflowers – they'd been cut about three days so were pretty fresh. I thought well, I've got to get rid of them. I made a space by the door, trimmed them and made them into a great big mountain. It was before supermarkets and if I had a greengrocer's shop now I'd put up a great big printed notice: 'There is no sell-by date in this shop. Everything is fresh every day.' I used to put little notes on the peaches: 'Don't squeeze me until I'm yours' and display red tomatoes in with the grapes, one here one there. It made them all look nice.

My head office, where I used to do all my phoning and administrative work, was in the King's Road, over my Chelsea shop. I called it The Greengrocer's Shop. Straight forward, no messing about and I used to interview managers there. They had to have personality, cleanliness and be trustworthy. I told them that if I found their finger in the till, I'd cut their hands off! They said I couldn't do that and I said I could. But if their till was right every day, I'd sack them. Why? 'Because with a busy shop you can't not make a mistake somewhere along the line.' I said, 'I don't look at the shillings and pounds. I look at the pennies.' I said I couldn't always be there, so at the end of the day they should pay all the takings into their local bank. Which they did, and most of them were very good.

I had one guy who had a contract with a mushroom grower down in Worcestershire – we had a good thing going there. He wanted me to supply London restaurants but I said there was already a firm doing that. Then I thought, well, there were plenty of restaurants and we could concentrate on the Chinese because they used lots of mushrooms. If he sent a load up to one of my shops, we could employ a driver to go round and get the orders. I asked him how many button mushrooms he could get: they were the number one with the Chinese. He said he could give me lorry loads of them. And he did.

One day Jennifer came to see me. I think she must have admired me for my get up and go (and good fruit!) but she only once came to see the shops. She came into the Chelsea one and said to my manager, 'Is Jonathan here?' He went 'Jonathan?' 'Yes,' she said 'this is his shop.' The manager said 'Just hold on a minute, madam'. He came up to see me and said, 'There's a woman downstairs and she's looking for a guy called Jonathan'. I said, 'All right, I'll come down' and I invited her up to the office. She said she was just passing, but that young man didn't seem to know me. I said, 'Well, they don't call me Jonathan here, it's John.' She was the only one who ever called me Jonathan. Sometimes at the end of the day, she'd say, 'You do look tired' and I'd say, 'Yes, well, it's hard work.'

When I had to pack it all in, I didn't actually sell my shops. I had to get rid of them.

Because I was in the King's Road, my customers had plenty of money and wanted the best there was. I used to meet a lot of influential people if they wanted something special for a dinner party. I'd buy a lot of Continental food for them like peppers and avocadoes, and kiwi fruits were coming into the country at that time. They all had to be

52

ripe and ready to eat and it was by order only, so I wasn't stuck with anything.

One day a guy came up to see me. He had a house in Lots Road in Chelsea and was managing director of a big company. He was having a dinner party and my manager had told him to, 'Go and talk to the guvnor'. We sat there chatting and I said I could deliver what he wanted a couple of days before he needed it. He introduced his friends to me to buy their stuff. He'd tell them, 'My greengrocer's a lovely man, get you anything you want.' One of them asked me if I knew anything about banking.

I said, 'No, only what I put in and take out.' He said, 'What about stocks and shares?' I said, no, I wasn't interested in them. He said, 'Well, you've heard of Lloyd's of London insurance company, haven't you? Great returns on your money.' I said, 'Like what?' He said, 'Well, have you got £1000 you could put in?' I said 'Yes, I could do that.' He said I'd get my money back in three months and my thousand pounds still lying there.

I thought I'd give it a try. He gave me an introduction and I put the money in. I thought that was better than my shops and I started throwing loads of money in. Everything I earned I put there, the returns were lovely.

Then came the Lloyd's crash. I had to pay £120,000 which meant selling everything: a big house in Chislehurst, all my shops. It ruined me. I went right back down to where I'd started. With nothing. A lot of people committed suicide because they'd put huge amounts of money in. The man who had talked me into doing it went the same way. Nobody saw it coming. It just happened overnight. A lot of people tried to go bankrupt. But that's no good for you in the future. The way I looked at it was I'd had it, enjoyed it and lost it.

But I always had my chair caning to fall back on, and that's what I had to do. Start all over again. I'm a gypsy, aren't I? I went back to my caravan that I'd always kept in a yard in Battersea. I've still got it. I've had to go back to caning five times in my life. I've always sat on pavements.

It was about this time that I started to play golf seriously.

Chapter 12

On the golf course.

I started playing golf when I was a boy in Mitcham. I used to have a walking stick and I'd go round the outside of the local golf club knocking stones about. An old boy used to sit on the seat there and watch me. 'Mmmm,' he'd murmur, 'very good.' He told me I had a natural swing and asked me how old I was. Thirteen, I said. Had I got a golf club? No, I hadn't. You couldn't join a golf club then, it was all toffee-nose, you know what I mean. 'You here tomorrow?' he asked. I said I came every day The next day, he brought me an old golf club made out of hickory wood. They used to make furniture out of it and tennis rackets and bows and arrows and things like that. He brought this for me and I've still got it. Funny old thing it is. 'Here y'are,' he said, 'and here's a golf ball. Come round the back here on the grass. It's quite long but you can practise your swing.' He turned out to be an ex-golfer and a golf teacher and was showing me how to do this, that and that. He told me I was a natural. My grandad used to say 'Where're you going now?' and I'd say to practise golf. 'You haven't got time to do that, get to work'. I used to have to take the golf club with me. But I got good, I'm right and left-handed and now my handicap is four with my right, and eighteen with the left. I did try to get into a couple of clubs but in them days it was a gentleman's game, you know what I mean. It wasn't until the 60s or 70s that lots of clubs started coming out and I've been a member of the Rotherfield club for about thirty years now. I used to play there during the week because Sundays they all go with their Rolls Royces and I don't mix with them. At one time, we played Mondays and Fridays. I'd go there come rain or shine, but then I thought this is a game not a punishment. I don't want to get soaking wet.

I've always enjoyed playing golf, it's a challenge, you're trying to do better than what you did last time. We've got an Irishman, lovely man, he's been with our golf society for about twenty years. I think he owned nine or ten pubs up in London. A really happy-go-lucky guy. The first time I met him – it was about eighteen years ago – he was standing there and I said, 'Someone late'? He said, 'Oim not waiting for anyone' (in lovely Irish brogue). 'Oim on me own.' 'Looking to play?' I invited him to come round with me. He was pretty good. He asked what my handicap was? I said six. 'Be Jesus,' he said 'the way you're hitting that ball' (admiringly). It was going straight down the middle about 150 yards. The next one was on the green in three. So we went upstairs and had a little drink. He said he'd just moved to the area and liked his golf. I asked him why he didn't join the club, and he said he didn't know anyone. I said well you know me, I'll introduce you. He liked to gamble. When I introduced him to my friends, I told them he was a nice guy but was keen on gambling. 'Well,' they said, 'we all like to have a shilling or two.' 'No, he wants pounds,' I told them.

I don't meet my golfing friends away from the golf course. I don't go round to their houses, but we do go on golfing holidays together and we've been to lots of places – Spain, Portugal, Morocco, Scotland, Ireland. The worst one was Dubai, it was too hot. The trouble is that in the summer season the time you go on holiday, it's much too hot to play. The Spanish have got the right idea. They open their clubs as soon as it gets light. It could be five in the morning. I think Ireland is my favourite place. They have beautiful golf courses. I know I'm a bit of a loner but I've enjoyed those trips – we can have a laugh and a joke.

Eight years ago, I had a set of golf clubs specially made for me. They cost over £2000. It was because of my swing. I was getting older and had to keep changing it slightly. Once you do that, you have to start all over again from scratch; you're not hitting the ball as you used to. I was talking to the pro one day and he said the only way to stop that was to have some clubs made to suit me. He said I should go to Bird and Sons in Wolverhampton. They were the best. You have to spend a weekend up there and get x-rayed. It's all done on the computer: they measure the weight of the clubs, their length. They look at your swing, the way you stand, they get your attitude to the game. Most pros have their clubs made there.

Chapter 13

*After the crash. Our villa in Spain. I take a local
council officer to court.*

I was fifty eight when I lost all my money and had to sell
my house and all my shops. I didn't have too much of a
problem. I went back to my caravan, and back to chair
caning.

I thought I'd try some villages in Kent but travelling
there every day from Battersea, made me think it would be
better to live in Tunbridge Wells. I'd already worked in a
lot of villages around there: Mayfield, Cranbrook,
Sissinghurst, Tenterden, in fact most Kent and Sussex
villages. Jennifer didn't like the idea at first because we
were getting on so well together. But when I explained to
her that I needed to make a living, she came round to the
idea. I told her that we would always be together at
weekends and I promised not to work on Saturday or
Sundays. They would be our days. Little did I know then,
it was 1988, how ill she was. She never said a word about
not feeling well. So I found a place to live in Tunbridge
Wells but was back with her some days and every
weekend. I still live in that flat.

Jennifer had a house in France that we used to go to.
One day she wasn't too well and didn't want to go there as
the Monte Carlo rally was on. She said she'd been told
about Marbella so we put the car, her 1985 Mercedes 2300
TE Estate automatic, on the boat, got off at Santander and
drove down to Burgos, where we stayed a night. It was
September and the next morning it was heavy with snow. I
thought driving was going to be a bit dodgy but didn't
know it was going to be anything like that. There was a
transport cafe nearby and a couple of lorries outside. I
thought I'd wait until one of them moved off and follow in
his tyre treads. And that's what I did. In Marbella, we

stayed in an expensive hotel. She liked the full business – having her hair and face done. One day we were going for a walk and she looked in an estate agent's window. I asked her what she was looking at and she said there was a nice villa for sale.

She went in and because she was a posh English lady they made a bit of a fuss of her. They got a guy to take us in a car to Gualamina. It was a beautiful house with swimming pool, lovely gardens. She asked me if I'd like to go and live there. 'Not really,' I said, 'I'm all right in England'. 'Well, we could have it as a holiday place', she said. She went down to the bank, got a banker's draft for the money – it was around 200,000 euros – and bought it. We used it a lot and had some good times there.

One day, back in England, I was sitting on the pavement in Haywards Heath and the sun was shining. I like it when the sun shines and it's easy. I went to the car in the car park to get a few chairs and when I got back three ladies were writing their names in my book. When I'm sitting in a place for the first time, I don't expect to get an order, just a bit of interest. I thought, I don't believe this. In fact, I got twelve orders that day and decided to go again next day. And I got another nineteen orders. I thought this is lovely, I've got a month's work. And if I can fill my book up in the summer, I won't have to sit out in the winter. No use sitting out in the rain.

A few days later I was sitting working there and a security man from the nearby pedestrian precinct came up and asked me what I was doing. It depends what these people are like. Sometimes I get a bit sarcastic and say, 'Well, I'm not waiting for a bus, am I?' This security man said, 'You can't sit here.' I said, 'I've been doing this for more years than you've been alive. I know what I can and can't do.' He said he'd call the police and I said they wouldn't be interested. He went away. All of a sudden a police car comes flying down the road and pulls up. 'What's up?' the policeman asked. Then he turned to the bloke who'd called him and told him not to bother him with silly things like this as they knew all about me, and he drove away.

Not satisfied with that, the security man phoned up the local council. I saw this bloke from the council standing across the road and looking at me. He came over. 'You got permission to sit there?' he asked. I said I didn't need permission. I asked him who he was, why was he questioning me and had he got identification? I knew they had to carry this with them but he didn't want to show it. I said 'If you don't want to show me your identification, just go away.' He put his hand in his back pocket and brought out his card. I've got a good memory, and remembered his name and number.

About an hour later he came back. 'Are you going to move from here?' he asked. I went, 'Well, no', and he said he'd call the police. I said, 'Don't do that, they're not interested and they've already been here once. They know all about me.' He came to me five times that day and asked if I was going to move. And each time I just told him to go away.

The last time he said he'd given me all the chances in the world and had asked me to go away, politely but I wouldn't go. I said, 'You don't really want to upset me, do you?' And he said 'Are you threatening me?' I said, 'No I'm just telling you. I've got your name and number and am taking you to court.' He said I couldn't do that and I said, 'Oh yes, I could.' 'What for?' he asked. 'Harassment,' I said. 'I've explained everything. But before I do that I'm going to give you one more chance' and I brought out the Pedlars' Act of 1871 that tells me what I can and can't do. I am allowed to sit on the pavement and take orders but I'm not allowed to trade.

What I was doing was showing people my craft and getting orders. The Pedlar's Act is a chartered law, it can't be changed, but it can be added to. For instance, if there is a shop window behind me, I have to be 18ft or 20 ft away from it so people can get behind me to look in it. I need a pedlars' licence but not a hawker's because I'm not peddling or hawking anything. I can take orders, but I can't take money. It's a very interesting thing to read. I have a copy from the library – Jennifer helped me a lot with this.

We were talking about it one evening and I explained to her what it was all about but that I didn't know how to find out more about it. She said we could do this in the library and we spent a whole day there. Jennifer was reading and explaining things to me and we came across the word 'trading'. We looked that up in the Act. It said Trading: the buying and selling of goods and services. Pedlar: a travelling trader who sells small goods.'

It turned out that I did none of these things. I only sit in the street doing my craft so people can see how it's done. Looking more closely at the Act, it said that I didn't need a certificate for getting orders for my work. I did all my trading in the privacy of people's homes, not on the street. So from that day on I realised I no longer needed a pedlar's certificate to do my work on the streets.

I told the council officer to read this Pedlar's Act but he said he didn't have to read anything and knew what he was doing.

So I went to the council offices, all suited and booted, and told them the story. They obviously didn't know anything about the Act and asked if I was allowed to sit on the pavement. I thought I wasn't going to get anywhere telling them about it and said I was going to take their man to court. What for? they asked. I told them 'harassment'. Well, they said, there was no need for that, but I said there *was* need. He'd got to be taught a lesson and know what a chair caner can and cannot do.

I went to a local solicitor whom Jennifer knew and explained it to him. He said, 'Well, I never' and was all for it. He said it would cost me money and I said never mind how much it would cost. I was ninety nine per cent certain I'd win. I said I'd pay him and give him his solicitor's fee from the court. The case was heard in Haywards Heath magistrates' court and it went like this:

John Lee to magistrate: I want to ask the council officer a few questions. Is that all right?'

Magistrate: Yes.

John Lee to council officer: Did I or did I not tell you or show you the Pedlar's Act of 1871 and did you refuse to look at it? Yes or no, please.

Council officer: Yes.

John Lee: Why did you refuse to look at it?

Council officer: Because I have all the paperwork I need in my office.

John Lee: But you haven't got a copy of the Pedlar's Act 1871 or you wouldn't have bothered me.

Magistrate to the council officer's solicitor: Has your client got the Pedlar's Act 1871?

Solicitor: Yes, here it is.

Magistrate to council officer: Did Mr. Lee show you this piece of paper? Did you not read it?

Council officer: No, I've got all that in my office.

Magistrate|: Have you got this in your office?

Council officer: Well, not exactly.

We won the case.

John Lee to magistrate: Could I have another word please?

Magistrate: Yes.

John Lee: I've won the case, so can I have my solicitor's fees from the council?

Magistrate: Yes, you have won.

John Lee: I'd just like my solicitor's fees, please.

Magistrate (*laughed*): You're a bit saucy but yes, OK.

John Lee: Could I also have payment for loss of earning as well?

Magistrate (*laughed*): Don't push it, Mr. Lee.

John Lee: Well, I have lost a day's money.

Magistrate: Yes, but you fought a case and won it, be satisfied.

John Lee: OK.

Strangely enough, one Sunday morning some four or

five years ago I'd been asked by a woman in Steyning to cane some of her chairs. It turned out that I'd done some for her mother in Chelsea many years before. She gave me permission to sit where I was and lo and behold, there was this council bloke. He'd got transferred from Haywards Heath. I saw him looking at me and I waved. He came over and said, 'Well, you're here now.' And I said, 'Yes, and I have permission from this lady to sit here so don't let me have to take you to court again.' I never saw him from that day to this.

Chapter 14

Jennifer dies

In 1989 Jennifer I had been together nearly twenty five years and I used to pop in and see her several times a week to make sure she was all right. I was working not far away at that time. One day I found her sitting on the settee and there were bruises on her face. I said, 'What on earth have you done? Who's done this to you?' 'Oh', she said, 'I was having a bath this morning and I fell over when I was getting out.' 'Did you faint or go giddy?' I asked. She said she went giddy. 'Did you call the doctor?'

She had, and he was coming that evening. She went privately. I said, 'OK I'll wait with you.' I asked her if it had ever happened before. She said she often came over faint but had never fallen down like that. 'I went out completely.' One of the maids had knocked on the door because she'd been in the bath a long time and she (the maid) wanted to make sure everything was all right.

The doctor came, examined her and asked some questions. Then he said he wanted her to go into hospital for a complete examination. She said she wasn't going there on her own and wanted a private room for me to go with her. The doctor said that could be arranged and he called an ambulance straight away. He was very concerned. I went with her and stayed the night. It was St. Thomas's in London – she had a lovely room and was well looked after. I went back every night to see her; I didn't want to leave her on her own. I knew she didn't like that.

She used to like me to read to her. I was reading a lot better than I used to, pronouncing words as they should be. She liked Frank Yerby's *The Foxes of Harrow* and I'd read that to her about four times. It was a big thick book about cotton workers in the South, Alabama way. She liked Ken Follett, too.

One day the doctor called me in. He said, 'I've got some bad news for you. Have you been together for a long time?' I said, 'Yes, nearly 25 years.' He asked me if I was next of kin, if her affairs were in order. I said I wasn't next of kin but that, of course, her affairs were in order. I thought it was a strange question to ask me. He said he didn't know whether to tell her or not. I said if it's something bad, don't tell her. She's not that kind of person. He said, 'Well, we've given her a good examination. She has a tumour on the brain that's too big to operate on.' I asked what he was trying to tell me? He said she had no more than six weeks to live. I said, 'Don't tell her'. He asked me how I would handle it? I said well, I'd tell her what we'd do when she got better. She has a villa in Spain and I'd say when she felt like it we'd go out and stay there. The doctor said, 'Are you sure you can handle this?' And I said 'Yes, but she should go home and have her own things around her.' He asked if she would agree to a live-in nurse and I said I'd ask her.

So I told her that she wasn't very well and that she had to be well looked after and the doctor wanted her to have a live-in nurse. She said there was plenty of room for that, and asked me what I thought. I said, 'Well, I think it's a good idea so that if you do get bad she'll know what to do. It will be comforting for you as although I've got a lot of common sense, I don't know too much about medical things.'

The nurse came to live in and Jennifer asked me if I would stay too. I used to read to her every afternoon and she'd fall asleep. One afternoon I went in and she said she just wanted me to give her a cuddle. She was in bed, it was about 3 o'clock in the afternoon. I lay next to her and she said, 'Talk to me, tell me what's going to happen when I'm better.' So I said what we'd do and wouldn't do. The next thing I knew was that she didn't look right. I couldn't feel the pulse in her neck or a heart beat. I pushed the button by her bed and said to the nurse, 'I think she's gone.' She said, 'She has'. I closed her eyes and she had passed away, just like that.

That was the way she died. I went to the funeral on my own. It was in Windsor where they had a family plot. There were a lot of people and her two children but they weren't close to her. I'd met her in my thirties and she had completely changed my life. She wanted to marry me but I knew it wouldn't work, my life was so different.

I went into a bit of a 'why has this happened to me' state? I couldn't get my head round it at first but then I thought she died peacefully, happily and that was it. She was seventy. She had been so much part of my life and I missed her a lot. But I told myself, I had to get on with things. When the will was being read out, I realised for the first time that she had put the villa in Gualamina in my name and the family's, which was a surprise. The son's face dropped: he thought his mother would have left it to him and wanted me to buy his half or sell it and give him the money. But I said I'd sell when I was ready. The solicitor said there was no urgency. She left me £100,000 but the family contested it, which I expected. They got a solicitor to say I was a gigolo only after their mother's money. But I didn't want the money. I wouldn't have known what to do with it. I got £50,000 and little bits of jewellery. I said to the solicitor, 'Don't write a cheque out to me. I want you to write it to Great Ormond Street Children's Hospital.' He asked what name he should put on it, and I said, 'Send it anonymously.' The only thing I kept was the car she bought me – the 1985 123 ET Mercedes Estate automatic and quite rare. I put it away last week for the winter. It has to be looked after. It is a beautiful car.

When everything that had to be done, was done, I felt I needed some space and time to be on my own. The only way I could find this comfort was to travel, just like my gypsy upbringing. So I went to the Cotswolds and was away for two years, staying on caravan sites and living as close to my gypsy life as possible. And this did give me a great feeling of satisfaction and belonging.

Chapter 15

A restaurant in Spain. The chief of police. A hidden microphone.

It was about two years after Jennifer's death when I'd been travelling and caning chairs in the Cotswolds, that I thought I'd go out to Spain for a while.

I hired a car and when I arrived at the airport in Spain, a fella's case burst open next to me. I offered to take him where he wanted to go which was the Marbella Club. When we got there he said he owed me a supper and why didn't I join him that evening? He was meeting some business friends who had come to look for a property to open a restaurant.

We kept in touch and a few months later they asked me if I would be interested in owning a quarter share of the restaurant they'd chosen to buy. I said not really, there was a lot of work to do on it. Then I thought, why not? I had money in Jennifer's villa that I could sell, so I said yes.

I went over there and found out what needed doing. We went to a solicitor and agreed I should have a quarter share. It was a big place – it could seat two hundred people, with space for a piano and tables on a balcony. But there was a lot to do to it and it was a year before we opened. We had a man in uniform on the door and you couldn't get a table unless you'd reserved one. We had chefs from France, Spain and Italy. Customers had to wear a tie and dress properly.

Our first customer was a tall, elegant man. He asked if he could reserve a table for twelve. His name was Foley. We didn't find out until later that he was Lord Foley, connected with the stationery company and well known as a pianist. We had a very good piano and he asked if he could try it. He played beautifully. All his friends came that night and they drank nothing but champagne and had oysters flown in from California. Afterwards he said it was lovely food, a great restaurant and he would come often. In fact he used to come twice a week and always played the piano, light classical. He played music from *The Glass Mountain* which I love. Because I had worked on cruise boats, I knew how things had to be done in a restaurant. I told the new waiters that they should stand by his table but not near enough to hear the conversation.

After the first year, we were doing well and I had earned a nice bit. We had a lot of regular customers, the British ambassador to the King of Spain among them. If you want a first class restaurant you have to have the right people, and I talked to the other partners about improvements we could make. 'What about the car park?' I asked. I suggested we should have a man at the door to drive customers' cars there from the restaurant. When it rains, it rains.

Two of us were always on duty in the restaurant each night, and one evening a waiter came over to me and said he thought there might be a bit of trouble at the door. I went to see. There were three men and one of them said he was the chief of police and wanted something to eat. I asked if he had reserved a table.

'No,' he said. I told him he had to reserve at least three days in advance. He said he was coming in. I said he wasn't. He asked me if I knew who he was. I said, 'I am English. English people don't make threats. We have a first class restaurant here with some famous customers. 'Like who?' he asked. 'Do you know that man over there?' I said, 'He's the British Ambassador to the King of Spain. There are Lord and Lady Foley. If you want a table, you reserve one.' He said, 'You think you are king of Marbella.' I said 'No, I own a high class restaurant. Can you see anyone not wearing a tie?'

The next time he came he booked a table and turned up with his wife and eight guests. I told the head waiter if he had any problems with them he should let me know. 'Keep an eye on them', I said.

They were making a lot of noise and I went over and asked this chief of police if I could have a word with him away from the table. I told him there were no rowdy people there except for them and if they didn't keep the noise down, they wouldn't be able to come again.

He said, 'You're saucy', and I said I was big enough to be saucy. At the end of the meal, he told the waiter to send the bill to his office. I went over to his table again and said I didn't want to embarrass him in front of his friends, but I'd like a little chat with him in my office. I told him, 'You have ordered and eaten food here, you must pay for it now.' He said he hadn't got the cash but that he'd like to have a chat with me which could be beneficial to both of us. 'Are you on duty tomorrow?' I asked. 'I'll meet you in a cafe and you can pay me in cash.'

One of our staff was a big Moroccan, a quiet man, gentle speaker, but he could kill you if he wanted to. I decided to take him with me. I told my partners what I was doing and they said I should be careful.

The next day I went to the café with the Moroccan. I had a red flower like a carnation in my buttonhole. In fact, it was hiding a microphone and I had a cassette tape in my pocket. I saw two men standing around and thought they must be with the chief of police. What he didn't know was that the tape was connected to my office, I knew someone with a radio shop who did burglar alarms, and he helped me do it.

The chief of police gave me a brown envelope with the money for his meal the previous night. I opened it, it was £25 short. I said we'd let that go but what did he want to talk to me about?

He said I could contribute to a police magazine each month. It was for businessmen. I knew there was no such thing. I said, 'You want me to pay you every month?' I realised it was for protection. 'I can make things a bit bad for you,' he said. I asked him if he was threatening me. 'No, I'm not threatening you, I'm just telling you.' I said that in England that would be threatening, I had no

69

intention of paying him protection money. He asked me if I'd like another drink. I said no thanks.

'I think we understand each other,' he said. I asked him when he wanted his first brown envelope. He said he'd come down and pick it up next Friday and have a meal in the restaurant. 'Are you going to pay for it?' I asked, not very hopefully. 'You mean you want a meal for nothing and I pay you for protection?'

He was starting to get a bit annoyed. I love it when this happens because then people make mistakes. I asked him who those two fellas were. He said they were with him. I said, 'You see that big fella over there? He's with me.' He said he wondered why he wasn't sitting at a table. 'You're not what you seem,' he said, 'But I think we understand each other.'

'Before you go,' I told him, 'I have a little present for you. You don't seem to be a bad chap and I can understand you now.' He asked what the present was. 'I have a tape for you,' I said, 'with all our conversation in the last hour'.

He was so cocky. 'I wondered about that flower and if it was hiding a microphone,' he said. 'But that doesn't mean a thing. I can destroy it and then what have you got?' 'What I've got,' I said, 'is that this tape is for you but I have another one recording in my office.'

'That's not possible,' he said. 'Anything electronic is possible,' I told him. 'And if I have any more trouble from you, and if you try and book a table in my restaurant, I will go to my solicitor with the tape.' He knew the solicitor – he was the prosecuting counsel against the police for another case. They were always at loggerheads and didn't like each other. The solicitor was quite a powerful man. He cost us a lot of money, but we needed him.

'You're rather clever,' he said. I told him I was just protecting my friends. 'What about the bill for this cafe?' he asked. I said he could pay that. I got up to go and saw the two blokes make a move so did my Moroccan.

I told my partners what I had done and gave them each a copy of the tape. I'd had three made. They were a bit worried about it and said perhaps we should have paid the bribe to the police chief. But I told them once you start doing that it never ends. He would take over the restaurant, make changes and it would ruin the restaurant. But I did realise this wouldn't be the end of it. If you made a chief of police look stupid, he wouldn't take that lying down.

A couple of months afterwards a Daimler in the car park caught fire. It must have been the police. I thought this was the beginning. Another night, about 10 o'clock, the lights in the restaurant went out. We had a generator so this didn't affect anyone, but it did cause problems. Another time, our kitchen caught fire in the middle of the night.

I thought this was not going to stop, the police could falsify our papers. I didn't want to lose all the money I'd put in, it was all I had. I'd lost it all once and didn't want to do that again. I decided to sell my share in the restaurant to the others in the group and they were all right about this. I also knew that a chief of police's job was for four years, and if he didn't make money then, that was it.

That was the end of my Spanish restaurant. Two years later the other directors had so many problems they decided to close it.

Chapter 16

Beatrice, the hotel receptionist. Tina, my daughter, is born. No going back.

After selling my share of the Spanish restaurant I came back to my flat in Tunbridge Wells and to caning chairs. This has always brought me a living and I've worked in villages and towns all over Kent and Sussex. About thirteen years ago now I decided I needed a little holiday and went down by coach through France to Spain. I'd arranged to stay at a hotel in Lloret de Mar.

I don't like hotel food – I like to get dressed up and find a good restaurant. I always take five or six suits with me, even on holiday. I speak a little Spanish and asked Beatrice, the hotel receptionist if she could give me a list of the best restaurants in the area. She told me there was a fish restaurant, which was rather expensive but top class food. I found the restaurant and it was a beautiful place. I had one of the best salmon I've ever had in my life. I had a couple of drinks, got back to the hotel around 12.30, made myself a cup of tea and went to sleep.

The next day I went to a flower shop and bought a bunch of flowers for Beatrice. 'That was a beautiful restaurant you told me about, and these flowers are to thank you.' The next restaurant she told me about was in the mountains and that I'd need a taxi to get there. She asked if I'd like her to book a table for Friday night. I looked at her hand. No wedding ring, no engagement ring. I said, 'When is your day off?' She said she'd got the complete day off on Friday.

I said 'I don't know you and you don't know me, and I don't know what your boyfriend will say about it, but would you like to come to the restaurant with me?' She said she hadn't got a boyfriend and yes, she would like to come.

It was a restaurant with home cooking and a view you could see for miles. I had the equivalent of steak and kidney pie. The pastry just melted in my mouth. After that I used to take her out every evening. She'd come from Alicante to work in the hotel. She was twenty six, much less than half my age. I was seventy four.

When I came back to England, I used to phone her and we wrote to each other. I went back once to the same hotel for Christmas and after that I went out about four times a year. One day she phoned me to say she was going back home and would I like to come and meet her parents? Her parents lived in the country. They were agricultural workers, very nice people, as I thought then. I was ten years older than her mother, twelve years older than her father. I stayed there a week.

Six months later she phoned to say she'd like to come to live in England as she'd never been. I said she could stay in my flat. It was two weeks before Christmas – about twelve years ago now – and when she arrived at Gatwick it was snowing. She'd never seen snow before and was like a little kid. She told me she'd have to find a job. I'd done some chairs for the manager at a local hotel and he said he had room for a receptionist. She got the job.

We were getting on well and then one morning she got up and said we had to have a talk. I thought, oh dear, she's had enough. 'No, I don't want to go back home' she said, 'just listen. I'm pregnant.'

I was seventy seven years old. A DNA test is so degrading. If you can't trust a woman, you shouldn't have one. She said she had never been with another man, only me, and I believed her. I took her to the doctor and he confirmed it. She told her mother who was over the moon. Her father? He was different. I said to Beatrice, 'We have got to be grown up about this. I am in my seventies and don't know how long I will live. I don't want my daughter, (we knew it was a girl), growing up and when she's ten years old, she wouldn't have a Dad because I'd died. I want her born in Spain where she has family.' Beatrice said she would be idolised as all the rest in the family were boys.

I took her back home and, as I said, the mother was over the moon, but the father gave me a 'What have you done to my daughter?' look. He wanted his granddaughter to be pure Spanish. I stayed for a month to make sure everything was all right. I told Beatrice that if she could find a place to rent, I could visit her.

I went over when the baby was born and bought Beatrice a people-carrier to make travelling easier for her. I told her I would have to go back to England to work but that it would be better for her to stay with her family. Something I regret now but then I was over the moon – I loved the baby to pieces.

Things did not go well.

Tina is now nine years old but I don't feel welcome at their house. I bought her a pony which she rides to school. She likes dressing up, playing with her dolls. She had a little mark on her nose and I paid for it to be taken off with a laser. We used to talk on the phone every Sunday evening.

But the grandparents have been difficult and things have got worse. When I went last time, Beatrice met me at the airport and said we had to have a talk. I said there's plenty of time for that. I took them on holiday for ten days to a nice hotel. We found a lovely restaurant and the owner spoke a bit of English. He said he'd got something on the menu that most English didn't like, would I like to try it? He said it was his mother's recipe for cooking a sheep's head. It was absolutely beautiful. He told me I was the only English person who'd eaten it in his restaurant.

Then Beatrice told me that she felt she had to look to the future. 'You're more than twice my age,' she said, 'and I have to think about when you're not here.' She said she might want to get married and I said, 'What about our child? She loves me.'

I stayed there a week. We always used to sleep together in her father's house, but this time we slept in separate rooms. I thought, there's something going on and I asked Beatrice if she no longer wanted me to be ....I didn't know how to describe it. I've never been in that situation before when I had to explain things that way. I asked her if she just wanted me to be a platonic friend? She said, what's platonic? I said, no sex. And she said, yes.

I'd always sent Beatrice cards for birthdays, Christmas, and Valentine's Day but this year I didn't send her a Valentine card. She phoned a couple of days after and asked why I hadn't? I said we'd been lovers for sixteen years and we'd had a baby, but we were just friends now and things had to change.

Now I know I am not welcome there any more. If I want to see my daughter I will have to stay in a hotel and they will have to come to me because her father doesn't want me in his house and I don't want to be there. I do feel very upset about not being able to see Tina. She used to phone me every Sunday night but our phone calls have stopped. I wish now I'd never said she should be born and live in Spain.

Chapter 17

Skills my grandma taught me.

In my grandmother's time, people used to bring their chairs to her. They had lovely big Victorian furniture with cane seats and backs. And there were a lot of caners. There's still a lot of work and sometimes I get twelve orders a day. I now think that if I can fill my book in the summer, I haven't got to sit out in the rain in the winter.

When you're working in the street, you have to use a little bit of psychology. People ask if I've got a card and I say no, I don't have one. I tell them to read the notice on the back of the chair next to me. It says: *Master craftsman, chair caning, sea grass, rushing, put your name and address in my order book. Free collection, free delivery.* Then I ask if they have something they'd like me to do. If they have, I tell them the best thing is for them to put their name and address in my book and they can be sure of getting their work done. I ring them up that evening and make arrangements to go and see the chairs.

One day I went down to Winchester because I had my caravan there in Old Alresford, one of my favourite places. When the Winchester bypass was built, they left three villages untouched: Old Alresford, New Alresford and Bentley. I was sitting in a little hamlet near there when this lady came up and spoke to me. 'I have some chairs I'd like you to look at,' she said. 'It's hard to find a caner where I live.' I told her I'd got a good map and she gave me directions. I went down on a Sunday and there were the big white gates she'd described, the white fence and a road covered in ceramic tiles. It was a beautiful house with a stream running by and a little bridge. I thought this was charming. I knocked on the door. 'Oh yes,' she said, 'I've got some nice chairs'. I looked at them and realised they were too valuable to take on the street. I told her I wouldn't like to be responsible for them and could I work on them in her house. 'Certainly,' she said.

I put a dust sheet down and started cleaning them. I always take a flask for tea and I'd been there about an hour when I happened to look across the field and saw two blokes walking across in suits. I thought that was a bit unusual. Farmers don't dress up like that. The owner of the house came out and asked me if I'd come inside for a moment, there was a bit of a problem. She said she had something to tell me and I said I'd got something to tell her too. 'There's blokes walking across the fields in suits,' I told her, 'and that's a bit unusual, isn't it?' She said that's what she had to tell me. I asked her if there was a problem, and did she want me to go and ask them what they were doing?

'No,' she said, and she told me that they were security guards for her husband, Sir John Glover. He was the colonel-in-chief of the Royal Green Jackets in Winchester, and had taken over when the previous colonel of the regiment was shot in Ireland. A white van parked up the road today was making the security men anxious and she'd had a phone call from them about it. In fact, the van belonged to a decorator who'd broken down and had now been cleared.

She was such a nice person. She had two cheque books and never gave me the one that said Lady Glover on it. A real coincidence about all this was that when I was working in South Kensington some years before, I'd done work for Sir John Glover's father.

Another time I was in Old Alresford again. I was sitting outside an antique shop when a policeman came up and asked if everything was all right. I said everything was fine. A couple of days after this he said he'd had a bit of a complaint. 'About me?' I asked, 'Yes,' he said, 'the man in the antique shop behind me doesn't want you to sit there.' I said he can't stop me, and he said yes, he knew that but to keep everyone happy, if he found me another place to sit, would I move? He found me a place and I was happy there. A lot depends on the way people put things, doesn't it?

One day a lady came out of a beautiful cottage just past the village pond. 'Come in a minute', she said, 'I've got two chairs I'd like you to see.' She went upstairs and looked down from the landing. 'Can you catch this?' she asked, about to throw one of them down to me. I called, 'Don't throw it. I'll come and pick it up. Don't throw that chair'. She asked why. I could see it was a delicate Chippendale. She said she had two of them and I told her to let me handle them. 'Do you know what they are?' I asked. 'Not really,' she replied. 'An old lady left them to me in her will.' I told her they were Chippendale chairs, about three hundred years old and valued at £6000 a pair. I told her I wasn't going to take them on the street. Anyone who knew anything about chairs, would know what they were straight away and if I had to leave them for a minute, they'd be stolen. Straight away. I told her they were very, very valuable and had she got them insured? She hadn't. 'Well,' I said, 'go down today and get them insured. They are not even chairs you'd sit on. They're 18th century show chairs.'

Chapter 18

Once a Romany.

It's always bugged me that, because my father wasn't a Romany, I could never be a proper gypsy. But I have remained very close to my traditions and tried to live that way. The things that have always helped me a lot are old sayings. I've lived the whole of my life by them and they are so true: never disturb a hornet's nest, let sleeping dogs lie, only tell people what you want them to know, one in the hand is better than two in the bush. My favourites are: if you've got no socks, you can't pull them up, and if you don't try, you don't get.

I'm a bit more settled now than I used to be. I once thought I would like to live in a little cottage with a garden where I could grow things, but now I feel content that I have my flat with a garage that I can use for a workshop. It's close to shops, the doctor and other things you need when you're older, and the nearby towns and villages are good for work. I think I'm always looking for something I can't have and I do get a bit lonely sometimes. Nice women come up to me when I'm caning chairs in the street but they're all married and I don't like to step on anyone's toes! I've got used to my own company, really. And I've still got lots of work. I recently had fourteen orders in ten days. Orders like that will see me through the winter when I'm not so keen on working outside.

I meet interesting people and have good conversations though sometimes I do know more about the chairs than their owners. Once a man was sure one of his was a Chippendale but it was only a reproduction, I didn't like to tell him.

I think I've lived a charmed life, because of Jennifer really. I couldn't read or write before I met her. She sent me to school and I'd never have gone on all them holidays in France and Spain. I never knew anything about opera. I got an education that I didn't have in the first place. I didn't talk like I'm talking now but when I go on a gypsy site and talk the Romany language, they still understand me.

I think about my grandparents very often and what a good life I had when they were both alive. I have beautiful memories of them. I remember how every evening my grandma would have her own 'quiet time' as she called it. She'd sit smoking her clay pipe on the steps of the *vada* with her shawl round her shoulders and have her 'thinking time' look on her face. She taught me a lot about life. What my real mother did to me and the family could never be spoken about but never forgotten. My grandmother knew I was going to have to live differently when she and my grandfather passed on, and she did her very best to have me ready for this.

I used to think my grandfather was rather hard towards me, but in later life I realised that his actions, too, were to prepare me for how I was going to have to live. He brought me up to be a man and not suffer fools gladly and was always testing me. One of his sayings was 'Let your eyes be your guide and your money the last thing you part with.' I loved them both dearly.

A happy life? It's been very challenging. Would I have done things differently? I'd not have invested in Lloyd's, that's for sure! I think what I'd most like now is for people to understand the Romany way of life, to look at Romanies with open minds and try to understand that they've been living the same way for hundreds of years.

Lightning Source UK Ltd.
Milton Keynes UK
UKOW02f1302011116

286627UK00002B/3/P